THE IRISH GAME ANGLER'S ANTHOLOGY

THE IRISH
GAME ANGLER'S
ANTHOLOGY

Edited by Niall Fallon

COUNTRY
HOUSE

Published in 1991 by
Town House and Country House
42 Morehampton Road
Donnybrook
Dublin 4

British Library Cataloguing in Publication Data available

ISBN: 0−946172−26−9

Acknowledgements
The author has sought permission of the following publishers, writers and literary
representatives to use copyright material, and is grateful for their responses:

Country Life for extract from *Going Fishing* by Negley Farson; J V Luce, FTCD,
for extracts from *Fishing and Thinking* by A A Luce; Eric Craigie for extracts
from *Irish Sporting Sketches*; Colin Smythe & Co. for extracts from *A Man May
Fish* by T H Kingsmill Moore; Faber and Faber for extracts from *Fishing Fact or
Fantasy* and *Fishing Fortunes and Misfortunes*, both by G D Luard, and for 'Trout'
by Seamus Heaney; Ziroon Ltd for extracts from *A Life by the Boyne* by Jim
Reynolds; Barrie Jenkins for extracts from *Wanderings with a Fly Rod* by Edward
Durand; Hutchinson for extracts from *A Sportsman Looks at Éire* by J B
Drought.

In the event of an inadvertent omission or error, please contact the publishers.

Text and cover design: Bill Murphy
Typeset by Printset & Design Ltd, Dublin
Printed in Ireland by Colour Books, Dublin

To my angling brother, Padraic; and to the salmon of Carrigacunna

CONTENTS

INTRODUCTION

The history of Irish angling literature is a strange one. Whereas other angling countries have made something of a fetish of their angling writers, we in Ireland do perversely the opposite; we hide them, we publish them sparsely, and then secrete their books so that only the most persistent of searchers can discover them.

It is difficult to say how much of this is due to a sense of self-effacing inferiority. But I have little doubt thay my own case is more or less typical. I had read the works of Skues, Halford, Sheringham and J W Hills before I had ever heard of O'Gorman, Peard or Kingsmill Moore. To my shame, I even fished with Kingsmill Moore in Connemara, unaware of his fame, or that he had written a book on fishing in Ireland. It was years before I realised that my late uncle's good friend, Dick Harris, crustily benevolent behind the counter of that wonderful and now vanished tackle shop, Garnetts & Keegan's, was none other than J R Harris of *An Angler's Entomology*.

In my formative years as an angler during the fifties, the angling literature I read was predominantly English, topped up now and then with scraps from America. *The Angling Times* was a weekly event in our household and therein I drank deeply of a strange mixture of floats and gentles, long-trotting, Allcock Aeriels and Mr Crabtree. I grew familiar with the great coarse waters of Britain — the Hampshire Avon, the Norfolk Broads, the Ouse and the Stour. I could discourse knowledgeably on bleak, dace, carp and chub, none of which I had ever seen, let alone caught. In short, while my practical angling education was wholly Irish, the academic side of that education was ineluctably British.

Irish angling writers came to me at a slow crawl. Occasionally I came across fleeting, but tantalising references to O'Gorman, Barker or Peard. I became intrigued. Like a prospector for gold, I scented a fortune of delight. I began to dig.

Slowly the nuggets began to reveal themselves. Kingsmill Moore was the first (and, in many ways, the best). Then came Luce, strangely under-rated. A friend bought a copy of Barker for me, and gradually but inexorably, the other authors seeped into my life.

And what is it like, this corporate body of angling writers? For one thing, it is sizeable. How sizeable I cannot say with finality;

but there are certainly well over one hundred books which deal wholly or partially with angling in Ireland. A high proportion were not written by Irish anglers, but by authors from England, and further afield, who spent fishing holidays in Ireland. However, the solid heart of our angling literature is indisputably Irish — O'Gorman, Kingsmill Moore, Dick Harris, Luce, Gwynn, Greendrake, Gaffey.

If the heart of our angling literature is Irish, the body is not wholly so. It is composed largely of English anglers who came principally to fish the western rivers and lakes, primarily for salmon, but also for brown trout and sea trout. In many ways, this well-trodden route has given rise to equally well-trodden experiences; as a result, there is a certain repetitive quality in many of the accounts.

But there is extreme richness too, much of it little-known and thus neglected as angling literature. Dr Walter Peard's *A Year of Liberty*, which describes a spring, summer and autumn tour of the cream of Ireland's fisheries in 1867, is relatively well known but still mostly unavailable (a reprinted edition is on the way). It remains a lively, well-written, diverting and revealing account of Irish angling in halcyon times. Some of the fishing which Peard enjoyed verges on the outrageous, almost the unbelievable; in particular, the trout fishing was of majestic quality and proportion.

F D Barker, born and brought up with a variety of fishing in America, discovered County Clare when living in England and thus began a love affair which lasted for many years and culminated in a rare and delightful angling classic *An Angler's Paradise*, published in 1929 and shortly to be reprinted. Barker concealed the object of his particular angling affection, the region around the town of Corofin and Lough Inchiquin, by giving fictitious names and altering maps. He had as his boatmen and advisers the famous Egan family of Corofin, headed by the wonderfully drawn Patsey, who boated for him on 'Inchicrag' for many years. Later on, in his declining years, Barker built himself a house beside Inchiquin. A true love affair.

Barker, like Peard, enjoyed wonderful fishing. Then as now Inchiquin, its surrounding lakes and River Fergus, could be dour, but the quality of the fish caught then could not be repeated today. Inchiquin is still an excellent fishing lake and the Fergus is one of our finest limestone streams, but some of the days and nights which

Barker and Patsey experienced are mere dreams for the rest of us.

G D Luard had something of Barker's instinct for secrecy (how like an angler not to give away his best fishing!). His *Fishing Fact or Fantasy* and *Fishing Fortunes and Misfortunes* are by no means great literature but they paint a lovingly evocative and accurate account of fishing in deepest rural Ireland during the first half of this century. As with Barker and his 'Inchicrag', Luard christened his anonymous angling kingdom 'The Big River' and 'The Little River'. On both, he spent many years' holidays, from a schoolboy to an old man, with 'Dick', his great friend and owner of 'The Big House, Ballyhimmock'.

Curiously enough, the location and characters of Luard's books remained a mystery for many years until Dr Jean-Pierre Poux, that fine French angler, member of the eccentric and exclusive Fario Club of the late and great Charles Ritz and, not least, lover of the difficult trout of the Tipperary Suir, persuaded me to solve it.

In the end, it proved simple enough; 'Dick' turned out to be one Richard Grove Annesley, landed gentleman, gardener, angler, hunter and shot; 'The Big River' and 'The Little River' became the Cork Blackwater and its lovely tributary, the Awbeg, where Edmund Spenser once lived. And Ballyhimmock, cleverly disguised by Luard, was the beautiful Annesgrove near Castletownroche, Co. Cork, whose woodland gardens were created by 'Dick' and which are now open to the public to wander in and admire.

Luard's writing has a quality of involved belonging, a running thread of enthusiastic and simple love of angling and the places it brings the angler; this sense permeates his books much as it does those of BB (Denys Watkins-Pitchford). The two Luard books — and he wrote another very good one on his angling experiences in North America — remain for me at the centre of Irish angling writing, evoking that indefinable and loose quality of Irish fishing, where organisation is absent, where nothing ever turns out as planned, where fun is forever threatening the serious.

On a higher plane of literature, however, is my own personal favourite: Stephen Gwynn, Member of Parliament, writer and lover of Ireland. Gwynn, let it be said at once, had severe shortcomings as an all-round game angler. The art of dry-fly fishing for trout remained always at a distance from his sphere of angling accomplishment, which is hardly surprising in one whose fishing was learned amongst the spate streams and hill lochs of Donegal, where a half-pound trout was a triumphant crown to a day on the water. By his own account, he was clumsy with fish and tackle, so much so that he referred always to himself as being a duffer; and indeed based perhaps his best book, *Duffer's Luck* on his own evaluation of himself.

But what a writer Gwynn was! — lyrically descriptive, sparely dramatic, hysterically funny. Three extracts in this book, picked almost at random, illustrate to perfection those distinct traits; *In Connemara* is a simple account of an idle row in the gloaming of western Ireland; *The Sway of Corrib* describes an intense and absorbing battle with a great trout; and *Sprite on the Slaney*, though I have read it a hundred times, still makes me laugh.

Like Luard, Gwynn remained emotionally rooted in Ireland. Both men had travelled, fished and lived elsewhere; they must have been entirely opposite characters, yet their books have a curious linking of mutual love of Ireland and its fishing, and a keen sense of the ridiculous. They can, and do, laugh at themselves as anglers must.

Humour was a quality shared by two of the earlier writers on Irish angling. O'Gorman and Greendrake/Greydrake wrote two seminal works which, although showing wide differences in knowledge, approach and experience, nevertheless harmonise well together in giving us a strong taste of what angling was like in Ireland in the early part of the 19th century. O'Gorman's *The Practice of Angling* and Greendrake's *Angling Excursions* are rarely met with these days and cost a small fortune from antiquarian booksellers; but they remain as charming and lucid descriptions of a bygone age. We do not know who they were; even O'Gorman's first name is a mystery, while Greendrake and Greydrake were, we know, pseudonymns for one J Goad. There is much to research here.

Although first published as late as 1931, and lately republished through the enthusiasm of Colin Laurie McKelvie, S B Wilkinson's *Reminiscences of Sport in Ireland* again is notable for its vivid portrayal of the 19th century and the early part of this century. Wilkinson was an engineer whose job took him to the more remote and wild parts of the west of Ireland, particularly to the north-west. There was little for him to do other than shoot and fish, and luckily for him he loved both. He enjoyed a quality of sport which we can only envy; his book is filled with tales of battles with big salmon and great bags of birds, of day after day of superb sport sustained by whiskey and peat fires. Wilkinson was no writer but his energy and vivacity shine through every page of this splendid book.

Much the same love of sport, the same ability to laugh at one's misfortunes, the same modesty, are displayed by Laurie Gaffey, who wrote two little-known books some fifty years ago. *A Freelance Angler in Ireland* and *Freshwater Fishing in Ireland* are over-ambitiously titled; they are, in fact, descriptions of Gaffey's own fishing days, most of them spent within a few miles of Dublin. What makes them memorable in some minute but unmistakeable fashion is the love which runs through them like a vital vein of life. This lends Gaffey's otherwise flat and jumpy writing a liveliness and interest, and more especially a humour best expressed perhaps in his description of a day when everything went wrong — a day that every angler knows full well.

T H Kingsmill Moore, judge, angler, writer, humanitarian, is widely and properly regarded as the finest writer on Irish angling. I am perhaps the sole exception to this popular opinion, for I feel that Stephen Gwynn shades the great man by a whisker. And why? Because Gwynn was a man whom angling had to some extent humbled; he could make mistakes and admit to them; he had shortcomings and knew it. Kingsmill Moore was a great man and a great angler but he did not suffer fools at all, let alone gladly, and there are in his book few instances of the failures and the foolishnesses which beset all anglers.

But what an angler and a thinker Kingsmill Moore was — an Irish Skues who brought a similarly acute and logical mind to the proper analysis of angling problems. His knowledge of sea-trout angling and of that strange fish and its ways was as comprehensive as it was illuminating; he appeared to have a facility for seeing into the mind of the sea trout, of divining their quirky whims. And he wrote divinely well, almost as well as Stephen Gwynn.

Where Kingsmill Moore surpasses Gwynn, however, is in a superior analytical way. Gwynn was robust and honest, an old-fashioned angler who rarely theorised but got on with what he was doing and enjoyed it hugely. Kingsmill Moore, on the other hand, approached the problems of angling determined to solve them through logic and invention. That he succeeded is evident; his sea trout flies are amongst the finest and most successful still used —

the Kingsmill, the Bruisers, the Bumbles. His writings on the fisheries of Connemara remain definitive blueprints.

I fished a couple of times with Kingsmill Moore, both times by accident. The first time was on the Corrib, when he arrived to find no boat awaiting him. I was nearby, a young man with a boat but without either boatman or partner. 'Partner?' said The Judge, 'I'll partner you — and you boat me.' So he did and I did. I had never, to my shame, heard of him as an angler but knew of his public reputation as a humanitarian, espousing all sorts of good causes. We finished and he talked; he was a good and kindly man.

The second time was at Delphi, a few years later. I had dropped by in the hope of a day on Doolough but the fishery was booked out. Kingsmill Moore was on his way out the door to fish Finlough. He recognised me and as he was short of a partner we fished together. He was older and noticeably more frail, but the talk was as stimulating and ceaseless as ever. All I remember of the angling was that I used a small Claret and Mallard to greater effect than he used his own creations; but he would not change.

We never met again, other than once or twice socially, but before his death our paths crossed in a curious way. I was fishing the Corrib with a boatman who is now dead and for one reason or another, the talk came around to Kingsmill Moore. Did he know him? Begod he did — sure didn't the Ould Judge give him a reel, and didn't he have the same reel with him in the boat that day. He produced it, a well-worn Hardy salmon Uniqua, and I bought it from him on the spot for a fiver. I have it in my study and I like to think it was the same reel that the great man used to catch four salmon one after the other from the Fairy Seat on the Slaney — that very incident described in this book.

Although A A Luce's *Fishing and Thinking* is not half as well known, nor indeed all that highly esteemed, I find it one of the best books on Irish angling that I have read. There is admittedly much in it which is philosophical and even obscure, but this should not be allowed to hide the fact that it is filled with close observation, shrewd analyses and diverting tales. Luce loved Lough Conn particularly and *Fishing and Thinking* contains the finest writing on that lake ever published.

Although it is not *per se* an Irish angling book, J R Harris's *An Angler's Entomology* is as good as being Irish. For years I had heard

14

of 'Dick' Harris as a good friend of my angling uncle Leo Maher, and had met Harris many times across the counter of that now defunct angling emporium, Garnetts and Keegan's of Dublin. But for some odd reason it took me years to connect that gruff but kindly presence with the man who wrote what is still the definitive work on angling entomology.

Although it is nearly forty years since his book was published, Harris remains indomitably alive in every sense, a man whose knowledge of fishing in Ireland is unequalled. Here is a real Skues and a Sawyer combined; sitting by the window of his house in Dublin, where he ties flies without the aid of glasses, he has solved my fishing problems with an almost dismissive ease. What a pity it is that Harris has not written a book on Irish fly-tyings, for no one knows more about the subject.

While these men comprise the body of those who have written more or less exclusively about Irish fishing, there is an even bigger body of angling writers who have included Ireland as a smaller part of their books. Both Sir Edward Grey and Maurice Headlam have written beautifully of the Suir and its difficult trout and I could omit neither of them from this anthology. Negley Farson dropped in to Ireland once or twice in his world travels, while a rarely seen work of John Bickerdyke's, *Wild Sports in Ireland* deals almost entirely with fishing and shooting on the Shannon — if you ever see a copy, buy it and treasure it.

Sir Thomas Grattan Esmonde was an international sportsman who caught salmon in British Columbia, shot moose in Alberta, wolves in Romania and kangaroo in Australia. He lived in Co. Wexford, my own home county, and owned a fishery on the Slaney, of which he wrote well and lovingly. His two books, *Hunting Memories* and *More Hunting Memories* have excellent bits and pieces in them, not the least of them concerning Lough Derg, where he dapped for many years for the great trout which are, alas, now very scarce there.

More centrally Irish are the works of the Rev. Henry Newlands and of Cosmopolite, otherwise R Allen. The latter made a trip to Ireland during the 19th century and later wrote of it cantankerously, outrageously and inaccurately in *The Sportsman in Ireland*. I find it amusing, annoying and entirely unbelievable — but read it you should. The Rev. Newlands' book *The Erne, its Legends and its Fly-Fishing,* is entirely different, dappled with the nostalgia of those great

15

years before the Erne was ruined in the cause of progress. A fine and romantic book, as is William Hamilton Maxwell's unforgettable *Wild Sports of the West* which, although it holds little enough of fishing, has enough to bring the reader back to it again and again.

Many anglers have sampled Irish fishing and wrote briefly of it before moving on. Edward Durand (*Wanderings with a Fly Rod*) wrote of the bog rivers of the midlands, still almost as unknown as they were in his time; British Army man Arthur Mainwaring was stationed in Ireland for a while and showed that he enjoyed thoroughly its fishing and its women, and not least its drinking (*Fishing and Philandering*); James Dickie in *From Tyrone to the Test* wrote perceptively of fishing both in the north and south of Ireland. There have been many others — Francis Francis, W Belton, Frederick Halford, Philip Geen, Joseph Adams, J B Drought, A W Long, Sidney Spencer, Brian Clarke, Sir Humphrey Davy, Hugh Falkus, J W Hills, and in latter years, David Street. And, I have no doubt, many more I've neglected.

Many are guide-type books, technical and topographical. They are too numerous to list but they include Edward Fahy, Colin Laurie McKelvie, Peter O'Reilly, Ken Whelan, Peter Brown, Michael Kennedy, T J Hanna, Hi-Regan (J J Dunne), William Matson, Augustus Grimble, W E Frost and M E Brown, E J Malone (the definitive work on Irish flies, *Irish Trout and Salmon Flies*). There have been others also, including some indescribably inaccurate so-called 'guides' — pity the angler who might use them as such.

From them all I have culled the meat of this book. If they have proved one thing to me at least, it is that Irish angling has had its chroniclers, perhaps not as many as in other countries but collectively managing to impart a good deal of the unique flavour of fishing in Ireland. Together they give a diverting and interesting view of a nation by lake and river, a nation in whose bountiful waters the salmon and trout continue to thrive. May future writers of these riches continue to thrive and give us more of the same.

Niall Fallon,
Hill of Down,
Co. Meath,
Ireland.

ODD CURRENTS

CHAPTER 1

Part of the diverse charm of angling is the unexpected, those events
and moments of eccentricity and oddity which befall all anglers.
Whether it is Major McVeigh's gigantic eels or (one of my own
favourites) Sprite missing the salmon on the Slaney, both of these
are an essential part of the twists and turns of an angling day.

Such days and such events are, of course, nothing without the
calming and illuminating element of humour, another prerequisite
if an angler is to remain sane through the years. Thus J B Drought
is able to smoke a pipe of solace when a young maiden shows
him up as a lesser fisherman; Negley Farson is able to swallow
an Irishman's rebuke for his impertinence, and the captain is
forced to endure the deceit of the 'Brown Caughlans'.

A LITTLE SWIM

When fishing in Connemara, in the summer of 1869, I started one morning very early from Glendalough Hotel, our headquarters, for the Snave Beg ('The Little Swim'), so called because it is the narrowest part of Ballinahinch Lake, in fact little more than a strait joining the upper to the lower lake. My wife and two children were, after their breakfast, to meet me there. By half-past nine I had killed two salmon, and in order to cast my fly over a fish that was rising a long way out, I stepped out from stone to stone on some slippery rocks. Just as I reached the point I was making for my feet went from under me, and I fell flat on my back into the lake. All my clothes, I need not say, required drying, so, as the sun was hot, I spread them on the rocks and ran about across the heather to warm and dry myself. While I was still in this unusual fishing costume I heard the sound of a car rapidly approaching, and saw, to my horror, that not only were my wife and children upon it, but also another lady. Fortunately there was a large rock close by; behind this I carefully concealed myself, and despatched one of my boatmen to stop the car, and to ask them to send me a rug and as many pins as they could muster. The rug was pinned round me, my arms left free, and my legs sufficiently so to allow me to walk, and thus attired I fished for three full hours, until my clothes were dry.

William Le Fanu, *Seventy Years of Irish Life*

As befitted his position and generation, the squire set great store by etiquette. "Always remember there is another angler in the boat". He taught us to imagine that there was a high perpendicular sheet of glass fixed athwart the boat, and extending out for some distance from the sides. This marked out the areas proper to each rod, both in the forward and backward casts, and if flies did not trespass outside their own areas there could be no tangling. A simpler way to avoid any possible tangling is to use a switch cast, which ensures that the flies never cross the line of the boat and has the further advantage that the flies are longer in the water. The only time when experienced fishermen occasionally get their lines tangled is when fishing a dry-fly in the twilight, and when this happens it is well to remember how far sound travels over water.

Consideration for the other angler also requires the direction of the boat's head to be changed frequently, especially when fishing a shore. Most anglers prefer to cast forehanded, with their arm free of the boat, and the cast nearer the shore is usually the better. I once asked the squire what he thought of a famous classical scholar who came from the neighbourhood. "Not much", he replied. "He always tried to take the inside cast."

T H Kingsmill Moore, *A Man May Fish*

THE DUKE'S DINNER

With reference to these black fish, writing of them recalls an amusing incident which happened to us some years ago, when, having brought home a gentleman of 42 lb., who for reasons best known to himself had gone into the deepest mourning, our host packed him off to a well-known owner of racehorses. The gift was warmly acknowledged, and in return we were sent the winner of the Cesarewitch, which happened to be in the stable of our friend. So far so good, for a few days later all of us were a little the richer. Now the big fish had been sent by our host because he knew his friend was not an angler, and would not attach much importance to the colour of the gift. Neither did he; but to our dismay, later on we heard that as he was leaving home, and could not eat it himself, he had presented it, "as one of the finest and best-conditioned fish he had ever seen," to a royal duke, who, well knowing all about salmon, was much too clever to eat it. Now, although the duke had also backed the winner of the Cesarewitch, he nevertheless vowed we had conspired to make an attack on his digestion, and that this was a matter that could only be put right by a meeting round the royal table under a solemn promise that we would drink as much "forty-seven" as the big fish would have wanted of water for him to swim in.

Augustus Grimble, *The Salmon Rivers of Ireland*

From *The Wild Swans at Coole* (1919)

'Although I can see him still,
The freckled man who goes
To a grey place on a hill
In grey Connemara clothes
At dawn to cast his flies,
It's long since I began
To call up to the eyes

This wise and simple man.
All day I'd looked in the face
What I had hoped 'twould be
To write for my own race
And the reality;
The living men that I hate,
The dead man that I loved,
The craven man in his seat,
The insolent unreproved,
And no knave brought to book
Who has won a drunken cheer,
The witty man and his joke
Aimed at the commonest ear,
The clever man who cries
The catch-cries of the clown,
The beating down of the wise
And great Art beaten down.

Maybe a twelvemonth since
Suddenly I began,
In scorn of this audience,
Imagining a man,
And his sun-freckled face,

And grey Connemara cloth,
Climbing up to a place
Where stone is dark under froth,
And the down-turn of his wrist
When the flies drop in the stream;
A man who does not exist,
A man who is but a dream;
And cried, 'Before I am old
I shall have written him one
Poem maybe as cold
And passionate as the dawn'.

W B Yeats, *The Wild Swans at Coole*

Opinionated, argumentative, knowledgeable, O'Gorman's book on the early days of Irish fly-fishing is one of the seminal works on the subject. Today, a rare copy costs hundreds of pounds.

A letter, of which the subjoined is a copy, has been sent me by the gentleman to whom it had been addressed; I give it without note or comment:

"Stamer Park, Ennis, April 20th, 1838.

"My dear sir — I find that O'Gorman is writing a treatise on angling, and has taken on himself to give prudential directions to the lovers of that delightful sport. Now, you shall see how well-qualified this Nimrod of the rivers and lakes has proved himself to direct or advise. What I am about to state, has occurred within a few days, and to my own knowledge.

"He had killed a large salmon on the Upper Fergus, which encouraged him to put a boat on it; his first day in the boat was dead fine, yet he had not fished long when he rose a large salmon (not a breath of wind!). 'Oh, said he, he won't take, but I will try him with a single-gut fly;' on looking at which, he observed the noose a little faulty; the rower desired him to retie it; — 'No,' said he, 'if he even rises, he will not take,' and down he threw the fly most exactly, and on raising his hand, had him fast. Away the fish went, showing himself, and shortly ran back. On wheeling up, the handle of the wheel turned on the axle, and now he is regularly beat; but he pulled in the line through the loops, which, when again running out, hitched; the salmon sprang out of the water, unravelled the noose, and took away the fly, which a few rounds of silk would have saved, as the link was not broken, but slipt — and the top of the rod was also smashed on the occasion. Here is a fellow to talk of Franklin's advice! Well, sir, the next day I met him with a broken rod, not spliced, only lapt together — the same wheel put in some way to rights. And here I must remark that he has two or three pet rods and wheels intended for an expedition somewhere that I can't guess at; but away he went with a fry to look for pike, not a mortal with him, and he had not been long out, when he got hold of a very large salmon, which quickly abstracted about ten yards of his line, which was actually cut by an old top loop which he neglected replacing by a new one. The day after, I went with him, and rowed him up the river; still the same lapt rod, the same wheel, but a new top loop, nothing but a salted fry for a bait. We had not got to the upper part of the river, when he called out — 'I have him!' — thinking him a large pike; but to my great delight, after a long race, it proved to be a very fine spring salmon, which we killed after great play. Then he says, — 'If there is a salmon in this next ford, I will rise him with a fly;' which he did, but for want of wind, the fish would not take.

"Now, sir, here is your famous angler, having good rods, using bad ones, not even spliced; bad wheels, bad lines, old sharp top loops, from sheer laziness not even tying or even knotting the noose of his fly; and I have learned from a bystander, that he lost, after sunset one day last week, another large fish and his fly, by some like neglect. I request you may show this letter to Counsellor Henn, who will be sure to abuse him as he deserves; and I hope you will not be wanting on the occasion; to conclude, he is a very neglectful, careless angler, though possessing great perseverance, with a very impatient, bad temper: indeed, I think he is the worst tempered angler I ever met.

"Believe me, my dear sir,
"Yours truly,
"M. FINUCANE.

"The Hon. John Plunkett."

O'Gorman, *The Practice of Angling*

The cream of the Erne season is from the middle of June to the middle of August. In the great year of 1881 —

Mr. L. Lutwych .... had 36 in 5 weeks.
Captain Gaussen .... „ 62 „ 11 „
Mr. R. Crawford .... „ 53 „ 53 „
Mr. E. P. Bates .... „ 68 „ 6 „
Mr. H. J. Simmonds .... „ 85 „ 6 „
Mr. C. Prescott .... „ 55 „ 4 „
Mr. T. Tatham .... „ 42 „ 4 „
Dr. Andrews .... „ 45 „ 3 „
Sir Ford North .... „ 43 „ 7 „

In the season of 1883 Mr. E. P. Bates made the highest recorded score of late years, as in five weeks he took no less than 114 fish, weighing 1100 lb., in which there was one splendid fellow of 52 lb.

In season 1885 —
Mr. Phipps Cooper .... had 58 in 5 weeks.
Mr. H. L. Kerr .... „ 40 „ 3 „
Mr. H. J. Simmonds .... „ 48 „ 8 „
Mr. E. P. Bates .... „ 79 „ 6 „
Captain Fullerton .... „ 53 „ 5 „

And then coming to more recent times —
Sir Henry B. Robertson .... had 29 in 2 weeks.
General Dickens .... „ 24 „ 2 „
Mr. E. P. Bates .... „ 43 „ 4 „
Mr. J. M. Somerville .... „ 45 „ 4 „
Mr. R. E. Graves .... „ 34 „ 4 „
Mr. J. Arkell .... „ 43 „ 3 „

In season 1895 —

Mr. J. Hone .... had 24 in 4 weeks, two of them over 20 lb., from the Ford and Moss Row.

Mr. J. G. Vokins .... had 22 in 3 weeks, one of 30 lb., from "Causan-na-Mhanaig" ("The wing above the flag").

In 1896 —

Mr. J. G. Vokins .... had 28 in 3 weeks.

Sir H. B. Robertson .... „ 33 „ 4 „

In 1897 —

Mr. T. M. Pike .... had 57 in 16 weeks, amongst them one of 36 lb., from "Laputa".

Sir H. B. Robertson .... had 18 in 3 weeks.

In 1900 —

Sir H. B. Robertson .... had 24 in 3 weeks.

Mr. T. M. Pike .... „ 31 „ 4 „

Mr. A. Marf .... „ 23 „ 4 „

Augustus Grimble, *The Salmon Rivers of Ireland*

Although the following is a tale of eels and not of trout or salmon, I am unable to resist its fascination — nor indeed its triumphant air of honour vindicated.

One afternoon in the late fifties, Major McVeigh came into my shop and while waiting for his order he overheard a chat between The Gael, Paddy Canty and Garda Egan about a big eel that had been caught in the traps at Newhaggard weir. At that time Mickey Brogan had the traps leased from Eddie Malone. The eel was estimated to be in excess of 7 lbs weight, but unfortunately, it had escaped when being taken from the eel house. It was so big it got its tail against the iron rim of the net which gave it sufficient leverage to burst its way through the sackings.

Major McVeigh then told a story of how his workers or their families would never go near one of the two lakes on the Drewstown estate, as the old people would tell stories of monsters being seen in it. Once when he was home on leave from India as a young officer, the herd at Drewstown poisoned some dogs that were worrying the sheep. As it was Spring and the ewes were yeigning, he was too busy to bury them, so he dumped them into the "haunted" lake. Some time afterwards, two monstrous eels were found floating on the surface of the water, dead.

When Major McVeigh described the size of the eels, there was a lot of laughter and wisecracks such as "give him the belt". (The belt was an imaginary Lonsdale Belt conferred on any person in the Trim area who spun the most atrocious yarn. It was usually won by an employee of either Smyths or Spicers!) This grand old gentleman who claimed to be a friend of the great T. E. Lawrence was so annoyed at their laughter that he asked them to meet him again the following morning. When he arrived the next day he was armed with a photograph complete with frame and picture cord and also carrying a diary. The photograph showed the McVeigh family, the butler and all the staff gathered around looking at two eels draped down the pillars of Drewstown House. The diary said the year was 1907 and the larger eel measured just over twelve feet, had a girth of twenty five inches and weighed forty one pounds. The other one was ten feet long, had a girth of nineteen inches and weighed twenty nine pounds.

The Irish record for a freshwater eel caught by rod and line is 6 lbs 15 ozs and the Irish record for a conger eel is 72 lbs caught by the same method. A couple of years ago there was a conger, weighing 112 lbs boated off the coast of Cornwall. It was also caught by rod and line.

Jim Reynolds, *A Life by the Boyne*

Stephen Gwynn was a lyricist of Irish angling. Here he is on the River Slaney in pastoral County Wexford, on a stretch owned by his friend Michael Sweetman, and outwitting the Sweetmans' indefatigable little terrier.

Another episode — but it has not the authentic touch of fame because I am the sole articulate witness — was the adventure of Sprite. Sprite was Michael Sweetman's Sealyham, and we met when I first came down to fish on Michael's water, and renew a friendship made in France. I suppose I was introduced to Sprite at the station, but I first became seriously aware of him when I hooked a salmon about the third or fourth cast. Nobody expects things to happen quite so quickly, and Michael and his gilly were gravely concerned about my methods, which they thought too drastic; while I was priding myself on bringing the fish to the gaff inside of a minute or two. Then suddenly there was a flop, and Sprite had gone for the salmon which I was heading to the bank.

Normally, the duty of any looker-on was to hold Sprite: I have gaffed a fish for Michael with him under my arm, palpitating like a motor car, and screaming like a soul in pain because he was not allowed to go and bite the salmon. When there was no spare hand on the bank, Sprite always went in. Once I believe in his zeal he bit through Michael's line, and more than once he caused the loss of fish. He was beaten, but the instinct was too strong: besides, Michael fostered it. He had brought back from India one of the fish wrought in brass scales which writhe all over when you shake them, and it was a regular game to make Sprite attack it when it wriggled. Once it lay still and dead on the floor he took no further interest: nor did he in your dead salmon, except that he would guard what had been caught under his auspices. But while the fish was still plunging, Sprite desired passionately to get his teeth in. Once, Michael, gaffing a fish for me, let it slip from the gaff on the bank, and hurriedly seized it by the tail. Sprite had the same idea an instant later, and it was Michael's finger that he bit. Michael, who was a just man, did not beat him then; he said it was his fault, and Sprite was within his rights. Indeed I am a little doubtful whether he ever really beat Sprite, and he never really had the heart to leave him behind.

I had, though, and used to shut him up when I went down by myself, but more than once he dodged me and sneaked along under cover. It happened so one day when there was a little flood on the river, but so late in August that one did not take fishing seriously. I saw him stealing down on the far side of a hedge, but thought no more and proceeded to fish Synnott's stream without any expectation — using light tackle and a very small fly, as one would in Donegal. And when the fish took, it was pretty far down and he was fairly heavy; still I got him in to the bank and was getting my gaff out, when splash! there was a small white object also in the water; Sprite in the midst of his rabbit-hunting had heard my reel go and seen the rod bent, and came valiantly to my assistance.

Now there was a pretty strong stream, and just below where I stood trying to gaff my fish, was a line of alder bushes, perhaps fifty yards long, with branches into the water, and the fish, scared by Sprite, had retired towards them. Even without the dog, I should have had difficulty in getting him up stream unless he wanted to come, and I saw no means at all to get hold of Sprite. Remonstrance was useless, Sprite was out to enjoy his hunt. So I took a resolution. The main stream ran a little outside the alders, and I turned the fish into it, and when he got out a few yards, I lifted to make him wallop on the top, and he did, and Sprite of course made straight for him. Equally of course, the fish headed fast down stream away from this new variety of otter. The alders had been cut, I held my rod high, and down we went in procession: the salmon with my fly in him, heading it, Sprite a couple of yards behind, paddling fiercely, and I legging it along the bank inside the bushes. There was a stile to climb, but I got over, and in that order we continued till the alder bush ended, and there was, as I knew, a back-water on my side. Into this I pulled the fish when he reached it. Sprite, carried by the stream, went away past us, and landed twenty yards farther down, and by that time I had whipped out my salmon. Undoubtedly the dog felt he had been done. He walked up the bank past me, and affected not to know there was a salmon there. Michael averred that Sprite did not like that matter mentioned to him for at least a fortnight.

Stephen Gwynn, *Duffer's Luck*

Arthur Mainwaring was a British officer stationed in Ireland in the early part of this century. Fishing clearly was not his only interest; his book is as full of pretty women as it is of fish and fishing, mostly on the Erne and on the Cork Blackwater.

Watching the river one sultry summer's day, it occurred to me that the reason fish refused to take in such weather might be because they were all half asleep like myself, and that possibly a brick-bat or two in their midst might make them sit up and take notice. This theory I ventilated in the "Field," incurring the usual derision that invariably greets any novelty of ideas.

On the day in question the Colonel and I started fishing in the Quarry Pool. For a quarter of an hour we fished most carefully, but then we had to stop, for a workman came to tell us they were about to explode a charge of dynamite in the quarry. Watching the blue smoke curling away from the fuse, I found myself wondering what the fish would think of the concussion, and remembered my own remarks on stirring them up. Now whether the workmen had put in an extra charge for our benefit I do not know, but the explosion seemed a mighty one as the huge rocks, riven from their hold, rose slowly into the air only to descend again into the field with a mighty thud. One block, at least twice the size of a man's head, fell with a thundering splash into the very middle of the river not forty yards from where we had been fishing. "Now is the time," quoth the Colonel, "to prove your precious theory." The ripples caused by this bolt from the blue had barely subsided as I made my next cast, and felt a pull at the shrimp. In another cast or two he came again, and I killed a fifteen pounder. *Verbum sap.*

A Mainwaring, *Fishing and Philandering*

G D Luard fished the Cork Blackwater and its tributary, the Awbeg (near the home of Spencer's faerie queen) for many years.

He stayed as a guest at Annesgrove, Castletownroche, County Cork, the ancestral home of his schoolfriend, Dick Grove Annesley. The family still live there in the gracious old house whose wonderful gardens in the valley of the little Awbeg are open to the public today.

He would dive down, too, after salmon fry caught and thrown back when trout-fishing, till only the stump of his tail was visible, and where the water was deeper he was sometimes completely submerged, remaining under for quite a long time, and hunting eagerly with wide open eyes beneath the water. Sometimes he caught one that was feeble, and then I regret to say he at once proceeded to scrunch and eat it. I'm afraid his tastes were a bit crude; certainly he thoroughly enjoyed a meal of raw fish fresh from the river, and probably this added to his sporting interest in them.

Once I made good use of this habit of his. One rather heavy and thundery day I was keeping an eye on the men haymaking by the side of the river, when I noticed several nice trout rising in the flat that bordered the meadow. Luckily I had my rod with me, but I had forgotten my landing-net.

I put on a biggish olive, and began with the lowest of them. He took it at once. The question was how to land him, for there was a line of rushes growing in the water about two yards out. Then I bethought me of Jock — I called to him and showed him the fish, now swaying on the top of the water, a nice trout of about three-quarters of a pound.

He caught on at once, plunged into the stream, seized the fish neatly in his teeth, and brought it ashore quite uninjured and without touching the cast, though I confess that once on shore I had to extract the fish from his jaws to prevent his making a meal of it.

Three more he landed for me and then the rise was over.

G D Luard, *Fishing Fortunes and Misfortunes*

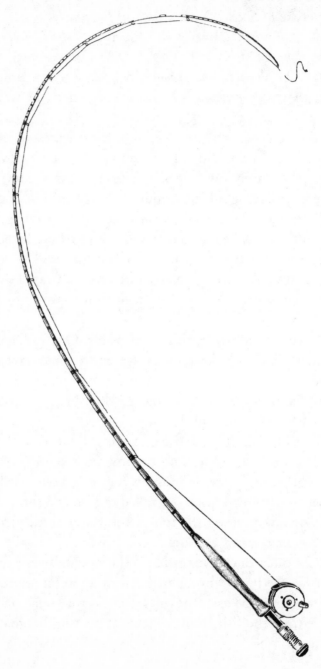

It is curious and regrettable that women anglers appear but spasmodically in Irish angling literature. Here, however, is the real thing, helping S B Wilkinson to land a big sea trout in wildest Mayo.

In the year 1908 I went over to Newport for a few days, and with the exception of the railway everything appeared just the same as when I left the place some thirty years before. I walked out one morning to see the spot from where I had hooked a fine sea trout; this was while I was living here and the tale is worth recording, showing how I gained by having a water keeper's wife on my side! I had got up early as there had been a nice spate and everything was perfection. About the second cast I was "in him," the trout making several desperate leaps and runs getting over a ridge of gravel into another pool and from which I felt I could never get him back and knew that he had me beat! The road and the river abutted and just at this time a country woman came along and "bid me the time of day" and after looking at me playing the trout saw the predicament that I was in, she said it was a bad business and asked if the fish was any size. I told her, as far as I could judge, from three pounds to four pounds — "a murdering pity" to lose such a good trout. Then she made this proposal: that she would take the rod and play the fish and when he was beat I might get a chance at him with the landing net. That was agreed to at once; it was the only chance and not much of a one at that. The woman took the rod out of my hands and I saw at once it was not the first time that she had played a trout. I proceeded to drop down from the wall about ten feet into about three feet of water running pretty swiftly, wading across to the far side of the stream. The fish could see me quite plainly and every time I approached it fled from one end of the pool to the other in very heavy water, making most determined rushes and "leps". The trout was now showing signs of being tired, and his big golden-looking body shining through the brown peaty water made me think that he might be a bigger one than I thought at first. After another run and jump it had shifted into another stream. Here the good lady "stuck the butt" well into the fish and led it beautifully up to and into the net. Such a beauty! I had to wade back to the river wall; everything my lady friend did was with precision: the way she wound up the line and laid the rod on the top of the wall *reel up*, then reached down for the handle of the landing net, pulling it up safely to the road; while I got out of the river bed, climbing up to the top of the wall in time to give a tap on what Dr. Peard in the "year of liberty" calls the "occiput." I had not scales with me, but on my return to my rooms was able to record that this sporting fish pulled the scales at five pounds good!

I thanked the good woman for having helped me and made her come in and have some breakfast and congratulated her on the masterful manner in which she had killed the fish. In reply she said: "Your honour, what about it? I have killed scores and scores of them in my time. Shure isn't me husband head water-keeper *up by*," meaning of the district. If all the water-keepers and their wives were such good sportsmen and women, using rod and line only (and no dragging of the pools with nets), there would be better fishing and I would never begrudge them a fish killed fairly.

S B Wilkinson, *Reminiscences of Sport in Ireland*

Oh! those Irish similes: if one could but remember them all or even a quarter of them. There was that prince of fishermen, Jack Douane, of Fermoy. I asked him to get me some worms to go salmon fishing. On going down to the stable yard over which he presided to get them, he turned them out for my inspection, as miserable a lot of gudgeon bait as ever I saw. "Why, Jack," said I, "what's the use of these wretched microbes; they're no use." "No use?" he exclaimed in a most aggrieved tone, as though I had asked him to lend me a shilling. "No use? I declare to goodness if ye don't get behind a bush when you're puttin' them on, the trout'll lep out and ate ye."

A Mainwaring, *Fishing and Philandering*

By three o'clock I had not seen a quiver of a decent trout. I had thrown back three or four of the variety called "tiddlers" and the breakfast mood of depression again had me in its grip. I vented it on Johnnie.

"Where are all these fine fish you were telling us about?" I asked. "I don't believe there's a decent fish in the river." He looked at me in pained surprise. "There's grand fish does be in it," he said. "It's no lies I'm telling ye, for I seen them same. Come with me and I'll put yez where ye'll play Puck with them." He discarded my flies for some home-made manufacture of his own, led me half a mile down stream to a natural dam above a long, dark pool and bade me cast across "the way the trouts would be coming up to meet ye."

Well, I did. I fished that pool, and several other pools as well, until my arms ached as severely as my temper. And I caught exactly three trout which, placed head to tail, might possibly have measured thirteen inches. Then from a little copse near by came Joan with what appeared to be the top and middle joints of an old salmon rod, spliced together with strong wire. In lieu of a reel, from the top joint hung a length of stout blind cord, to which was appended a salmon cast and a hook, baited with a peculiarly revolting worm.

"Hello," I said. "Where have you sprung from? You can't possibly fish with that contraption."

"Sez you!" replied the damsel in the disgusting vernacular of the rising generation. "You watch."

She dropped her loathesome bait into the water, squatted on her haunches on the bank and waited. But only for an instant. There was a boil in the water; a heavy splash, and the child sprang to her feet clutching the rod tightly in both hands, while almost simultaneously something described a parabola and hit the bank with a resounding smack six inches from my face. It was well both rod and tackle were of salmon-breaking strain, for that trout (and I lie not) turned the spring balance at an ounce under three pounds.

Johnnie once again had told the truth by accident; his wizened face was wreathed in smiles, though the fisherwoman was the least concerned of anyone. "I've caught them here before," she said, "but only little things. I dare say I shall never catch another quite as big as that." I shouldn't wonder if she spoke the truth. But when she pattered off, doubtless to dig up another close relation of that most disgusting worm, I laid down my rod gently, lit a pipe, and brooded darkly on the uncertainty of earthly things.

J B Drought, *A Sportsman Looks at Éire*

Negley Farson's delightful Going Fishing *is an angling classic the world over. This shrewd evocation of the crafty Kerryman O'Sullivan during the times of the Troubles in the twenties is, however, the sole reference to Ireland in the book.*

The six years when I was never in any one country for over six months, when I was living in Wagon-Lits and Ritzy or non-Ritzy hotels; when I was arguing with customs officials, concierges, and foreign chancellories around the world; when about the only things that ever caught up with me were my bills, were years, you would think, that held little chance for sport. Yet I saw to it that they provided just that thing. I believe that you do not learn much about any country by sitting in its capital. I had been some four months knocking about remote parts of Spain before I went to Madrid to see Primo de Rivera — and fishing with the Shetland drifters or over at Stornoway in the Hebrides taught me much more about the plight of the British herring industry than I could ever have dug out of the Ministry in London. So when I suggested to my paper that it would be a good thing to take my small round-nosed car and drive around the perimeter of Ireland — both the Free State and Ulster — so that Irish in the States might have some first-hand impressions of what it was like these days, my paper, being far-sighted, snapped at it.

It was not my fault that the Punchestown races were at Naas; that the Shelbourne in Dublin was full of perhaps the gayest collection of sporting people on earth; that I lost heavily on the races, and, in remorse, left the flesh-pots of Dublin — and poached every stream that I could, driving up the west coast of Ireland. In Connemara and in the Joyce country I got some most useful Irish politics that way. (But I got amazingly few fish!) At Dingle I lay over a few days to go off with the Irish 'nobbies' trawling in Bantry Bay. I lived with the captain of the little *Mary Immaculate,* and at night both he and his wife told me what the big steam trawlers were doing to all the little Irish fishing villages: 'Ruining us, they are!' said Captain O'Flaherty. 'Mind you,' said his wife, 'if it wasn't for the remittances coming back from America — sure Dingle itself wouldn't be here!' All the way out to the fishing grounds in the 'Nobby' Old John was down on his knees in our cabin, praying and counting his beads, for luck, and against the physical ordeal that lay ahead of him; for he was an old man, and he hung as if crucified on the warp getting in the trawl. The last day when a fog came down we saw the big grey shape of an Atlantic liner, her horn blowing, feeling her way past through the murk.

It was raining all the time, and the old man at the tiller waited until he got thoroughly drenched before he put on his yellow oilskins. 'Ah,' he said, 'I knew a man that trolled naked. Galway, he was. He took off his clothes and put himself into a bag. It had holes for his arms and legs.'

Commissioned by the *New York Sun*, in 1919, to write some articles on Sinn Féin, I deliberately used my trout rod as a bit of camouflage. At Killarney I got Mr. O'Sullivan, the butcher, to give me the lie of the land; where, in his judgment, was the best place to fish — were there streams handy? He took me out in his car, where he fell into a dissertation about trout.

'A delightful subject!' said Mr. O'Sullivan. 'It holds so many contradictions!'

'Are you one of those men who carry every fly in the world in their book — or do you chance it with just six or seven kinds?' I asked.

Mr. O'Sullivan stopped his car: 'I belong to the latter school. And I'll tell you why. . .'

'Is it true', I asked, 'that some of the lads were going to ambush a British lorry on its way to the Gap of Dunloe yesterday — only, the British took the wrong road by mistake?'

'Sure! and how the divvle did you hear about that? Mind you now . . . they were only Black and Tans . . . . t'would have been no loss.'

'I think I must have driven right past the lads in ambush?'

'Well, if you took that road yonder to the Gap of Dunloe — you certainly did. They was lying there all day. The British always take the wrong road.'

'I was lucky.'

''Twas not luck! Ye had the Major with ye. Nobody'll touch *him*. And you tell the Major we'll allow none of those Sinn Féiners from Cork to come over and burn down Flesk, either."

'Suppose you're reserving that burning for yourself?'

'Ah, shame on you. The Major's a Unionist — we know that better than he does. But he's no _____ absentee. Tell me (suspiciously) I thought you were talking about trout?'

'Personally,' I said quickly, 'I think a 9 ft. 3 in. rod is quite long enough. And a two-piece rod gives you a better action, doesn't it?'

'Ay — that's true. But you'll not be carryin' a two-piece rod about with you in a car.'

'No, you can't carry a two-piece rod about with you in a car. And especially in railway trains! Do the I.R.A. drill much in these parts?'

'I'll be getting back now,' said Mr. O'Sullivan; 'it's not trout ye have on your mind at all at all.'

Negley Farson, Going Fishing

THIM SALMON

An Englishman who goes over every year and rents a beat on the Lee was fishing below the Inniscarra weir one Easter holiday. Ardent and earnest fisherman as he was, his luck was out and he had not 'met with a fish' for several days and was getting slightly annoyed with the lack of sport, also with the endless succession of trout anglers coming along the banks from the city of Cork, on whom he looked with no sort of favour.

Presently one of these gentlemen strolled up the bank and stopped to watch him casting for a time.

"Would ye be tellin' me, sor, where I could be fishin' not to be pesthered by thim salmon?"

"What do you mean, pestered by salmon?"

"Well now, sor, it's the wan day of the year I do be fishin' and I started out with three casts; thim dam salmon have the two of thim whipt off me, and if they takes the other it's home I'll have to be going with niver a trout in me bag."

I leave you to imagine the Englishman's feelings, but I hope the recording angel was looking when he supplied the man with another cast, and a couple of trout flies, and told him to get on with the job.

W Durand, *Wanderings with a fly-rod*

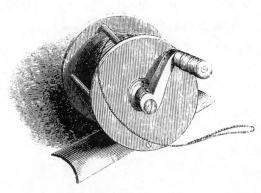

MISS PEACOCK

Eric Craigie has been one of Ireland's best-known sportsmen of the old school of huntin', shootin' and fishin' for all of his considerable years, much of it spent in his beloved Mayo.

The very first serious fishing holiday we had away from home followed an introduction from our bank manager, Mr Armstrong, to Miss Peacock of Maam Cross, who had four private lakes and kept a boarding-house. Her uncle, who attended all the visitors, was an alcoholic. She warned us that if her uncle ever suggested having a drink we must refuse. We spent all our time fly fishing from our boat and without a fish old Mr Peacock knew we were losing heart. One day he suggested we fish Mame, a small lake with very small fish; they would take the knots of the cast, he said. True to his word, we spent a glorious day catching fish less than a quarter of a pound. To crown it all, when the sun was setting and the light dimming, what flew across the lake but a pack of grouse. As quick as lightning my brother put up his gun and had a beautiful right and left which were quickly netted to the delight of old Peacock. This needed celebrating. Back to Peacock's pub, a pint each and in to dinner delighted with our day's outing.

Little did we know that Peacock locked himself into the pub when we left and drank himself silly. We knew nothing of the incident until Miss Peacock came to our room the following morning. Flinging our suitcases down the stairs she ordered us out. The woman was in no mood to be argued with. I really did feel ashamed when she kept shouting, 'You have broken the only rule I told you to be careful of.'

Eric Craigie, *Irish Sporting Sketches*

AN ANGLER IN SCHOOL

In the year 1826, my father having been appointed Dean of Emly and Rector of Abington, we left Dublin to live at Abington, in the county of Limerick. Here our education, except in French and English, which our father taught us, was entrusted to a private tutor, an elderly clergyman, Stinson by name, who let us learn just as much, or rather as little, as we pleased. For several hours every day this old gentleman sat with us in the schoolroom, when he was supposed to be engaged in teaching us classic lore, and invigorating our young minds by science; but being an enthusiastic disciple of old Isaak, he in reality spent the whole, or nearly the whole, time in tying flies for trout or salmon and in arranging his fishing gear, which he kept in a drawer before him. Soon after he had come to us, he had wisely taken the precaution of making us learn by heart several passages from Greek and Latin authors; and whenever our father's step was heard to approach the schoolroom, the flies were nimbly thrown into the drawer, and the old gentleman in his tremulous and nasal voice, would say, 'Now, Joseph, repeat that ode of Horace', or 'William, go on with that dialogue of Lucian'. These passages we never forgot, and though more than sixty years have passed, I can repeat as glibly as then the dialogue beginning, "η πάτερ οτα πέπονθα and others. As soon as our father's step was heard to recede, 'That will do,' said our preceptor; the drawer was reopened, and he at once returned, with renewed vigour, to his piscatory preparations, and we to our games. Fortunately my father's library was a large and good one; there my brother spent much of his time in poring over many a quaint and curious volume. As for me, under the guidance and instructions of our worthy tutor, I took too ardently to fishing to care for anything else. I still profit by those early lessons. I can to-day tie a trout or salmon fly as well as most men.

William Le Fanu, *Seventy Years of Irish Life*

He told me that it was quite a common thing for Lee salmon to take a trout fly. "When me ould dad was tying flies for ould Mister Haynes in Pathric Street, wasn't it the grand fly he was after inventing that would catch a salmon or a throut ondiscriminate: the 'Mystery Fly' he would be calling it. It's well I remember the time I was working in the shop with him as an errand boy, and me only knee-high to a shnipe. The English officers from above in the town would be coming in every day to be having a crack with him. Those were the days and thim were the lads; it's a sad day for Cork it was when thim same left.

"The ould dad was fond of his joke and the officers would be liking to hear the yarns he'd be telling them, and one of the lads would always be teasing the ould man about the flies he tied. 'Why can't you be tying them natral like?' says he. 'Them things aren't like anything that moves in the air above or in the waters beneath.'

"Well now, it's not much good the captain was at the trout fishing, and he would be blaming it all on the flies. One day he gives an order for half a dozen 'Brown Caughlans'. 'And tie them natral like so the throuts will be taking thim.' The dad niver says a word to him then, but that evening I sees him tying thim same and muttering to himself: 'Natral! I'll be larnin' him what's natral.'

"The next day the dad slips out for his pint of porther just whin the officers would be coming, and sure enough they comes in and starts asking for the ould man when I was minding the shop. Presently in he comes and 'Good morning, Sean,' says the captain. 'Have ye the "Brown Caughlans" tied for me?'

"'I have so,' sez he. 'They be hanging on a string in the window all ready for ye.' And himself walks over to get thim. 'Paddy,' sez he, 'have ye been moving thim flies I left here last night?'

"'I have not,' sez I.

"'Well now,' sez he, 'and that's the quare thing. I had thim same tied all ready overnight, and it's hanging on this string they were,' sez he, pointing to a bit of string across the window. 'Who has thim moved on me?' And he starts hunting all over the shop for thim same.

"The captain goes over to the window to help him look.

"'Is that one?' says he, pointing to an ould cobweb in the corner. 'Musha now, and it is, and here's another and another.' And he picks all six of thim flies from off the webs.

"The ould dad chuckles, 'Isn't it thim spiders that have the flies whipt off me? Now will ye be telling me thim same are on-natral? And the spiders thimselves not know the differ.'"

W Durand, *Wanderings with a fly-rod*

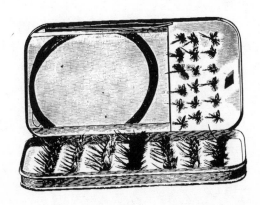

Another quite nice yarn was about another sportsman who had rented an expensive beat on one of the best known of the Irish rivers, and never touched a fish for the whole period of his lease until the very last day. "Then," Paddy went on, "by the grace of God and a big stick, he met with a fish at last. Sure and didn't he handle it as tinder as a piece of joolry, and when his man had it gaffed and on the bank, wasn't there the sorrow in his eye as he looked at it.

"'Shamus,' says he, 'do ye know that fish has cost me five hundred goulden sovereigns?'

"'Well, glory be to God, yer honour, and I hopes ye niver catches anither wan.' And Shamus was niver after knowing why the quality would be laughing at him."

W Durand, *Wanderings with a fly-rod*

Another local legend which I heard was a story of the late John Bright and his old fishing crony, Peabody, the philanthropist. They used to fish the Shannon, at Castle Connell, and one day they came up for a turn on the lough. Two of the chief boatmen of Killaloe joined forces, and did themselves the honour of rowing these distinguished visitors. And a severe day's work these rowers had, for their patrons trailed persistently for eight mortal hours, and "never a drop of the cratur had they brought with them"! Arrived at the landing-stage, late in the evening, there was the inevitable policeman on the bank. John Bright, accosting him, said, "What is the proper price to pay these boatmen, constable?" He replied, "Seven-and-sixpence, your honour; but some gentlemen give them ten shillings." John Bright, turning to his chum, said, "I have no change, Peabody; have you three half-crowns?" The millionaire produced the coins, and gave them to the boatman nearest to him. Holding them in the open palm of one hand, whilst slowly scratching his head with the other, he said, "And they calls ye Paybody, don't they? Well, I calls ye Pay-nobody."

G W Gedney, *Fishing Holidays*

49

THE GENUS GHILLIE

CHAPTER 2

He is (almost) always called Paddy, whether or not this is his real name. He is feckless, childishly eager, ready for anything, and fond of a drop. To the many foreign anglers who have come to Ireland, there is no one quite like him.

He is, of course, the Irish ghillie (rarely called that but more often referred to as a boatman). Like a fishing day, there are good and bad ghillies; not all are as wise and intuitive as Kingsmill Moore's Miley Costello, nor as scheming and astute as the immortal Jamesie ('ye should know by this, Jimmy McDonagh, that that was a thravellin' trout and wherever he is now he is not where he rose lasht'). But from Grattan Esmonde's dapping Danny to A A Luce's Paddy, Barker's Patsey, to 'poor Pat' on two shillings a day, the genus ghillie lends a rare flavour to angling in Ireland. Long may they lasht!

River fishing is a one-man pursuit, lake fishing a partnership. There may be a partnership of three, if the second rod is a friend with similar views, but the ideal is two: the angler and his boatman. The boatman supplies the knowledge of local conditions while the angler decides the method of fishing. It takes time to perfect such a partnership, for every angler has his own theories and methods, which necessitate the boat being handled in the way which suits his style, and the boatman must learn to do this without continual direction. Some boatmen will not learn and some try to dictate. The wise angler will accept suggestions from an intelligent boatman but he must never tolerate dictation.

I have had many fruitful partnerships but none so ideal as that with Miley Costello of Fermoyle. Speech was unnecessary, and indeed Miley seemed to have a mistrust of speech, doling out his rare remarks as if he was dispensing a dangerous medicine. It was a point of pride with him to be able to read the mind of his angler and take the appropriate action before he was told. Nothing escaped his observation. A turn of the head, a glance at the sky, a shift of position, the opening of a fly box, these gave him the clues to what was going on in my mind. Yet there must have been something more than quick observation. I would think "I wonder is the salmon which I saw move by the big rock last Saturday still in the same place?" and Miley would take up the oars and row me to the most favourable point for drifting the big rock. To fish with Miley was to have four eyes. Battling up against half a gale he would suddenly stop the boat and point out a direction for me to cast and as often as not the flies would be taken by a fish whose movement he had spotted despite the roughness of the wave. I can recall his making only one error, and then the real fault was mine. While he was away gathering heather for the luncheon fire the wind died and I changed to a thin and rather worn cast, but kept on the same flies. I was so accustomed to Miley seeing everything that I forgot to tell him about the change when he came back. As soon as we started again after lunch, a big white trout took the tail fly and charged straight in towards the boat. The orthodox counter is for the boatman to pull half a stroke, allow the fish's rush to take him past the stern and so avoiding the danger of a dropper catching on the keel. With any other angler Miley would have done this automatically, but he knew that with a cast of normal thickness I preferred to take in line with my hand and direct the fish by side pressure clear of the stern. The weak cast did not take the strain of so large a fish, and parted. Miley picked up the broken end, examined it and flushed. "To think I never noticed," was all he said.

T H Kingsmill Moore, *A Man May Fish*

"Sure now, and wasn't the ould earl the darlin' man, when so be it wasn't riled he was feeling. If it was so, glory be to God, but he had the words that would scald the feathers off a crow's back. It's well I remember the time when himself had the temper lost entirely, and thanks be to hivin it wasn't meself or the dad, who was with him, that he'd be cursing, but the salmon thimselves that wouldn't be after taking anything at all that day.

"There they were leppin' and flappin' in the water for ivery wan to be seeing, and divil the taste of a fly, or a shrimp, or even a worm, would they be taking for a whole week, and it's meself had all the three tried by the same token. Well now, the earl wouldn't be fishing with anything but a fly at all, it's poaching he'd be calling the others, but if so be the fish weren't rising bould, wouldn't he be telling the dad or meself to be putting up the spinning rod and trying the 'Colley' or the shrimp down the water behind him.

"He'd been after throwing the fly all morning, and it's himself could put a fly on the water fit to tempt an angel from hivin, but divil a fish could he meet with in any of the pools he tried. The dad had been watching him careful like, and he says to me: 'Now ye young omadhaun, ye be kaping out o' sight of himself, or it's withered ye'll be with the tongue of him. And don't ye be showing yerself 'till he has a fish cot, and by the hair of St. Padhraig it's careful ye'd better be after being with the gaff. By the houly saints, if ye miss your sthroke or break him, the Lord forgive you, cos himself won't and it's murther there'll be.'

"So I hides meself behind the bank the whilst he's fishing down 'Hall's Turn' and 'Parker's Gut'; and the language of him would have shut the mouth of Mother Moriarty, and her coming home from the fair-day, and by cripes, that same takes some doing and her with the drink taken.

"Well now, I'll be telling you that it got so bad that the dad creeps up to me and says: 'Himself will be after having a sthroke.'

But at that moment the ould earl opens his fly-book and, with a grand curse, hurls that and the rod both togither into the water.

" 'Isn't it ivery dom fly in the book I've tried ye with,' he bawls. 'Here, take the whole bloody lot and choose fer yerselves.' And he stamps away up the bank, cursing and swearing like the Ould Wan himself.

" 'Do ye fly down the river, Paddy, and cotch that book before it be schwept away entirely,' says the dad to me. 'And I'll be trying for the rod with the shrimp tackle.' And away I belts and sees it floating there in the flat below 'Parker's Gut,' and says a prayer that himself above on the bank won't see me schwimming out after it. And faith when I gets back, wasn't the dad up to his neck in the water after that same rod, and when he came out with it, and the two of us stood there with the water running out of our boots, wasn't it dhrowned entirely we were.

"While we were up at the farm changing, in stamps the earl. 'Holy murther, Sean,' he says to dad. 'I've thrown me book and me rod into the river.'

" 'And why wouldn't ye?' says me father, peaceable like, and he not knowing how the old gintleman's temper was.

" 'And I after wanting to be fishing again this afternoon.'

" 'Sure now and we have the both saved on you,' says me dad.

" 'God be good to ye, but that's grand hearing. It's a trifle annoyed I must have been to be doing the like.'

" 'By the holy cripes, if it's only a trifle annoyed ye were, may I be out o' hearing when it's real angry ye are.'

" 'Off with ye now, Paddy,' says the earl, 'and be bringing the waders. Haven't I fished this river for years from top to bottom, and don't I know every stone of it from Coolcour Bridge to Cork, and haven't I fished the whole countryside all me life, day and night, even to standing in the water after dark under the walls of Carrigadroghid Castle, and me wondering all the time when the "Pookha" would be catching me. And at my time o' life I'm not going to be beaten by these dom salmon, even if they do be making me lose me temper. Sean, I'll be fishing the "Wood Hole," and do ye be fishing the "Island Stream" and the "Orchard Turn" with that dom shrimp ye're always advisin'.'

"'I will so,' says me father. 'But it's heedful ye'll need to be of the "Wood Hole" with the water there is in it. The rain was black in the hills, and the Sullane and the Dripsey may be roaring down.'

"But divil a thing would he hear, and off he goes to the river, lickity split.

"I see him start in at the top end of the 'Wood Hole,' and it's wading down the bank side he was when I goes upstream to the dad, and him bawling for the shpinning rod. In thim days they did not have the road cut under the bank, that ye can fish the stream so, and that without wading. I was only with the dad a tin minutes or so, and wasn't I kaping an eye cocked that himself did not meet with a fish the whilst I was helping to whip on a shrimp, when suddenly we hears a terrible wallop in the water below.

"'My cripes!' says dad. 'And that's the biggest fish that ever lepped in the Lee.' And we looked down to see if himself had met with the salmon.

"Well now, I'm telling you, all we could see was a pother in the water, and two brogues sticking up above the surface.

"'Tis himself is drowned entirely,' bawls me father. 'Do ye be runnin' to the turn beyant, and shtick the gaff in him and he passin' ye in the shtream, and I'll be throwin' the shrimp to him, the way it'll be catching the waders.' And we both fled down the bank.

"But it was the ould earl himself that did all the saving, didn't he throw himself on his back and paddle himself ashore in the shallows below there as handy as a duck.

"'Sean,' sez he, and him lying on his back the way the water would be draining out of him, 'it's a judgment on me, it is, for losing me temper, but it's you and Paddy will be getting drowned saving the rod for me. It's there it is at the bottom of the river. I'm off to the farm to be drying meself.'

"And with that I pulls the waders off him, and away he tramps up the hill with the water running off him fast enough to be giving a duck the toothache.

"We gets the boat down from the flat above, and the divil and all of a time we has in getting it over the shallows and houlding it in the stream while I dives below for the rod. It's an hour and more we were before we gets the boat back above, the where himself would be wanting it to cross over home for the night, and just as we were walking down the bank, soaked to the bones of us, the earl comes down the hill as dry and jaunty as ye please, but looking odd about the legs and arms of him.

"Me father has one look at him as he comes up. 'Houly murther,' sez he, 'it's me best suit ye have, taken off me. How will I be getting to mass at all, and me with nothing to wear but me bare skin?'

" 'Sure, it's all right, Sean,' says the earl. 'Wasn't it herself above there at the farm who'd be giving it to me, to save me catching me death of could, she said. I'll be sending it back to-night, so as ye'll not be going naked to mass on the Lord's Day; and by the same token, I'll be paying for a new suit for you and Paddy there, for the wettings the two of ye have had the day.'

W Durand, *Wanderings with a fly-rod*

Dr Walter Peard's A Year of Liberty *was probably the first book to popularise angling in Ireland. Published in 1867, it portrays a fishing season enjoyed by the good doctor as he travelled around the best fishing spots in Ireland with family in tow.*

Your Irish attendant is a man *sui generis*; at least, there is nothing like him in our own land. Compare him with an English gamekeeper — be that functionary land rat or water rat — Pat is as much like him in body and mind as he is in dress, and in this particular there is no great degree of comparison. Our well-fed friend in neat velveteen, gaiters, and boots, stalks solemnly after you, as though he had reluctantly made up his mind to do a disagreeable duty. He shows not the smallest interest or pleasure in the business — neither exults at your success nor commiserates your failure, and pockets his half guinea with a silent touch of his hat and an aspect of being the most ill-used man in Christendom.

Now look on this picture of rags, hearty interest, indefatigable zeal, and active good humour, all for two shillings a day. If he cannot show you sport (and you may take your corporal oath he has done his best), he will tell you what might, could, would, should, or ought to be done — some of it truth, more, probably truth embellished. But with all his failings — and poor Pat is only a man after all — he is the best and pleasantest attendant, through heat or cold, hunger or thirst, in good fortune or evil fortune, that can be found out of his own tight little island.

With your florin in his hand, he bids "yer honor the best of sleap," says something hopeful about tomorrow, and with his duddeen in his mouth, and very little under his waistcoat, talks by his bit of smouldering turf for the hour together of what you did, he did, and they did.

W Peard, *A Year of Liberty*

I have often noticed that a good gillie will always carry your fish and never attempt to hide it in case a dog or human being might be on the prowl. This particular day my brother decided to fish up river and we were to fish down to the Junction Pool, a long walk. We had only started when I beached a nice fish. I suggested to Frank to put him in the drain and cover him with sods. He very reluctantly agreed. We had only fished a short distance downstream when we grassed another two fish and I had no trouble getting Frank to hide them in a drain running from the bog and covering them with sods.

We fished down to the Junction and there called it a day, knowing we had three fish to collect on our way back. When we came to the first hide the fish was gone, likewise the other two. Frank was full of temper. 'I told you the locals had eyes like hawks,' he said. I went into the sitting-room to find my brother happy and contented having a large Paddy.

'I only fished for half an hour and got three lovely fish. How did you do?' he asked.

'I killed three fish in the morning and when we came back to collect them they had disappeared.' (We always had a pound bet on who would have the largest bag.)

'Here, give me my pound,' he called. I parted with it reluctantly and went to the fish house where there were three fish on the slab. Frank came in and looked at the fish.

'They are mighty like our fish,' he said turning them over and over. 'Master Eric, I know how I gaffed your fish as sure as I'm McManoman. These are your fish.'

I went to my brother and told him what Frank had said. But no. He had killed one in Kane's Pool, one in Walsh's and the last fish by the lodge. I had no redress on my pound. My brother had a marvellous little bitch called Pip which always landed his trout and salmon. After an hour's fishing he had decided to give up and walk down to meet us. He had only gone a short distance down river when the bitch set. Thinking it was a badger he armed himself with stones and put Pip up the drain. She returned with a salmon in her mouth and then the other two fish. She had a marvellous nose and a mouth like velvet. I would never have had my pound returned only my brother was so anxious to let us know how good his little bitch Pip was. From that day to this Frank saw that each salmon was put into the fish bag and stayed there.

That was many years ago but I'm pleased to say that I still get much pleasure from the river, and much of it is thanks to Frank who taught me, my brothers and all our children to fish.

Eric Craigie, *Irish Sporting Sketches*

Here we meet one of Irish angling literature's enduring characters — F D Barker's Patsey on his beloved 'Inchicrag' (Lough Inchiquin near Corofin in County Clare) in the early years of this century.

At the time I first met him Patsey was somewhere about fifty years of age. Fully six feet in height, had he taken full advantage of his inches, he was broad of shoulder, but lean of figure. He looked like a man of great endurance rather than one of great strength. Patsey was a tireless oarsman, but a deceptive walker. If I would have his company on the road, I had constantly to slow down, and even then he would somehow get a step to the rear. But let him get you on to the crags, and you would find the relation reversed. Hour after hour over those broken, treacherous rocks, gun and game-bag weighing him down, he would go on and on until his companion, bathed in perspiration, was forced to beg for a rest.

His complexion had been ruddy, but exposure to sun and wind and rain had permanently browned it; when he removed his hat the broad expanse of exceeding whiteness came as a surprise. His hair, inordinately thick and already grizzled, he wore cut close to a well-shaped head. Originally it had been sandy, like his eyebrows and heavy, drooping moustache. His eyes were light blue and regarded one steadily as he spoke — kindly eyes, though lacking the humorous twinkle one finds so often in the eyes of his countrymen. What they lacked in humour they made up in steadfastness. Taken altogether his expression was gentle, but the long stubborn chin told its own story.

He spoke in a low, well-modulated voice, his words were well chosen, and I have never known him to utter a word of slang. Patsey was almost always serious, even when narrating events that convulsed his hearers with laughter; it may be that no small part of his success as a story-teller rested upon that sustained solemnity. 'I'll tell you a tale, sir,' meant that Patsey would soon have us all in a good humour, whatever had happened to put us out of it.

'The Pipe' was a great factor in Patsey's life. I learned to discover his humour from the way he filled it. When things were going well he was most deliberate in his preparations. The plug was first looked at; then the 'old knife' had a rub up on the gunwale of the boat. The cutting proceeded slowly, each fragment put carefully as it was cut into the hollow of his left hand, where in due time it was rubbed into consumable condition between his palms, while the 'old knife' was still retained between thumb and finger. Next the pipe was cleared and the dry crumbs placed on the new charge to facilitate ignition. Even then Patsey would dally with his gratification; survey his position, and pull a stroke or two before taking a match from his trouser pocket. The match might be struck on the oar or the thwart, but the favourite method was twice or thrice on the rough edge of the metal pipe-cover, so rapidly that the match crackled. When less tranquil than usual he would be less deliberate and burn more matches before the blue cloud arose and betokened that all was well. There followed a still more characteristic action with the pipe — to ease the draw he would hold the bowl inverted and strike it on the hard palm of his left hand with just two strokes — never more and never less — *'plunk, plunk'*. If there was a woman in the boat Patsey would go the livelong day without the solace of his pipe, until positively bidden to smoke.

Though an experienced fisher himself and quick to see an error, he was never over-free with advice. When he did venture to advise it was with great tact, and his suggestions were always worth consideration. How any one could resent his kindly advice I cannot imagine; yet one man did, and, as you might suppose, he was not a good fisherman. Patsey said no more — he devoted himself to pulling the boat and thinking — the gentleman fished in his own fashion and there were few trout in the boat that evening.

F D Barker, *An Angler's Paradise*

To the salmon angler a gillie is indispensable. The trout fisherman enjoys an independence which his brother in quest of larger game must forgo. The former, wandering along the banks of an unknown river, cannot well mistake the likely spots where trout lie, but a strange salmon river has few landmarks to indicate the habitat of *Salmo salar*. Besides, the impedimenta of gear and tackle require an attendant, and the gillie — patient beast of burden that he is — will shoulder everything in this way, and make light of it.

Every Irish gillie worthy of the name is an enthusiastic sportsman; he will drop the last or the plane for the sake of the sport which is the breath of his nostrils, and if he is attached to a reasonably-minded master will serve him with unflagging fidelity. He knows every stone in the river, has a keen eye for the conditions that make pools fishable, and will cast a fly with unerring accuracy to within an inch of the spot where a fish lies. Salmon-angling is hard work, but the gillie is never tired, and is always ready to mitigate the toil by taking a hand at the rod. He has a perfect talent for misleading his compatriot gillies when there is a rush for pools, and will tell Tim Sullivan that his governor is to be on the spot at 6 a.m., two hours later than the time arranged.

His poaching proclivities make him an early riser, and one must not complain if he is awakened at three o'clock instead of four by a shower of pebbles hurled at his dormitory window. To know that he has been a poacher is a commendable grace. It is generally alluded to as one of the cardinal virtues.

On one occasion, in summing up the merits of a new gillie, I was informed that he was the biggest poacher on the river, and with an air that showed that the vice was counted to him for righteousness. The accomplishment, however, has its drawbacks, and the poaching fever in the blood on occasion shows itself in ugly spots. Once I had arranged to fish a pool on Monday morning, which was full of salmon. The nets had been off from six o'clock on Saturday morning, and on Sunday afternoon the salmon were freely showing in the pool. At four o'clock the gillie was to call me. I awoke with a start at six, and, thinking that my attendant had overslept, I set out for the river. On calling at his house I was informed that he had started at daybreak, and was supposed to have gone in quest of me. I proceeded to the pool, and on reaching it found the gillie fishing with all his might!

But the principal vice is whiskey. This is even worse than the weakness for poaching. The free use of the flask on the part of English anglers robs many a fisherman of a valuable servant. The taste of liquor to these hot-headed Celts is like blood to the tiger. They will have more of it. One of the finest gillies I have known — a splendid fly-tyer and an out-and-out enthusiast — was lost to me for a week through lending him for a day to a brother angler. When he turned up again, full of apologies and regrets, I ventured to lecture him, and, with the best intentions of appealing to his better nature, asked, "Why do you touch it at all? You know the very taste of it means a week's drinking." But he was equal to the occasion, and replied, "Arrah, sir, it was a mistake altogether; I thought it was a bottle of Kops the gintleman offered me." Anglers, if they are to retain their men, must avoid offering them whiskey. Years ago a novel method of securing the gillie's sobriety is said to have been adopted on the Galway River. At the close of a day's fishing, the moment the gillie left the fishery he usually disappeared for two or three days for an obvious reason. The police-station was close to the river, and a constable was bribed to arrest the gillie the moment he passed through the gates. He was straightway taken to the guardroom and provided with a bed for the night. Thus his sobriety was assured.

When the gillie fails to turn up, drink, as a rule, is the explanation. His friends will assign plausible and even virtuous reasons for his disappearance. One, who was a carpenter by trade and an angler by profession, was missing one morning. The run of the grilse was at its height, and the prospects of a day's angling were unusually promising. I determined to hunt him up, and called at the house where he lived. His father opened the door, and when I inquired for Dan — which was not his name — I was informed that he was in bed. "Drinking again!" I ejaculated. "No, indeed, sir," came the reply, in a half-indignant tone; "the drink had nothing to do with it; he was up all night making a coffin." I hastily apologized and withdrew, meditating on the virtues of the man whom I had been mentally maligning. I had not gone far before I encountered the virtuous Dan emerging from a public-house in an advanced stage of intoxication. Evidently he had been up all night making his own coffin.

It is advisable to study this phase of the gillie's character to prevent being victimized by it. He is conscious of it himself, and by no means indisposed to enter into your plans for insuring sobriety. If one is fishing for three or four weeks a gillie's payment will amount to a considerable figure, and he will be ready to agree that payment should be deferred to the end of the engagement. Tips after a successful day's angling are dangerous. The attendant regards it in the light of an extra to be spent in a jubilant fashion. An angler will sometimes say, "Now, Dan, half a crown extra for every salmon we catch today." A crown may be due at the end of it, but no gillie will turn up next morning in all probability. It is far wiser to add all extras to the sum total at the end of the visit. I have known gillies who feared the danger of handling money during their engagement so much as to ask a local tradesman to be treasurer for them.

The optimism of the gillie is unbounded. The graphic description of the prospects, when one feels disposed to "chuck" sport after a series of bad days, is stimulating. "Where's the use," you exclaim, "in going on thrashing the river? The water is too low for a run of fish, and there is nothing in the pools but old stagers." "No run of fish! It's entirely mistaken you are, sir. Sure, when they want to come up the river it isn't the height they'd be mindin'. They'd travel if the river was dry when they set their mind to it; and, sure the pool by the wood is teemin' wid fish. I went down late last night, and they were so thick that you could

walk across the river on their backs without wettin' your boots!"
Then would come a touching appeal at the possible consequences
of wandering about the town and the temptations of the
public-house.

"It's yerself that's kept me sober for the last month, and the
divil a ha'penny o' pay I'll take today if I don't give ye a tight
line." Who could resist this? And the gillie will have his way in
the end.

After a blank couple of hours you feel disposed to comment
on the obdurateness of the fish. "They don't seem to be stirring,
Dan." "No, sir; there's thunder in air, and when it's like that
it's hard to move them; but it'll clear presently, and the rise will
come on at such a rate that if ye throw a copogue — Anglice,
dock leaf — to them they'd take it."

But, with all his faults, something like a genuine affection springs
up between master and man. There is no use in setting up a high
standard of consistency and expecting these gillies to conform to
it. To be a little blind to their follies is a wise course. The chances
are, from an angler's point of view, that the balance is in favour
of redeeming qualities. There is no prouder man than the gillie
when he leads the way to the hotel with a brace of fish slung
by the gills. He receives the tidings of your leaving with a look
of genuine regret, and, as he puts it, "will be counting the days
till yer honour returns. Sure, the sport ye've had is nothing to
what it'll be then, for this was the worst season ever known on
the river." He will be down in the morning to take the rods to
the station — "it isn't himself that'll be trusting them to them
divils of jarvies."

So he hovers round you to the end, insists on shaking hands
for the second time, and, as the train steams out of the station,
the last pathetic object standing on the platform and waving his
adieu is the person of the faithful gillie.

Joseph Adams, *Salmon and Trout Angling*

DAPPER DANNY

To the dapper a Danny is absolutely indispensable. The success or failure of your operations, the pleasure or otherwise of your experiences, depend mainly upon him. Your Danny is a good fairy in homespun. He does everything or thereabouts. He takes charge of you, protects you, teaches you, cheers you up, rejoices with you appropriately when the occasion arises, catches flies for you, puts up your rod, mends it when necessary, directs you as to the number of flies to mount, puts them on for you when you fumble with them, decides as to the weight of line to use, navigates your boat, hooks your fish sometimes; and, if you are wise, invariably lands them; lights your fire, boils your kettle, saves you from a watery death now and then, and generally does all things needful. And what your Danny does not know about the etiquette of dapping, of winds and waters, of where to go for trout, and what to do when you hook them, you certainly don't know, whoever else may.

On Lough Derg all the best people have Dannies. There are Dannies and Dannies, of course; but in my experience there is no Danny like my Danny. Year after year we have dapped almost unbrokenly, since we were boys together. We have had red-letter days of glorious sport. We have had many a bad day as well. But when the May-fly appears on Lough Derg we are inseparable; and when one season ends we look forward to the next; and we are both inclined to think that when our course is run, and the kindly Irish earth covers us over, we won't be completely happy, in that place to which all good fishermen go, if we can't still go dapping together.

Sir Thomas Grattan Esmonde, Hunting Memories

Jamesie was willing to be helpful, even forthcoming, in a discussion on flies, but when it came to the business of catching fish, he was a different man. He liked fishing, liked better to catch fish, but best of all he liked to show his superiority over rival boatmen. This was a necessity for his complete happiness. He would rather bring back a mediocre catch which was larger than that of any other boat, than a really good bag which only took second place. So far so good. Anyone fishing with Jamesie could be certain that he would leave nothing undone to get fish. But it did not end there. He craved also the personal triumph of beating the other rod in his own boat, and to make sure of this he was willing to use devious methods. He did draw a line. I have heard him refer with disapproval to leaving his companion's fly-box behind or weakening his gut by the touch of a cigarette. Physical interference was a foul, but when it came to a contest of wits anything was permissible.

It took me a couple of days to smell mischief. Most boatmen are only too glad to set the boat on a long straight drift and leave it so. Not Jamesie. From the bow came a continual murmur of directions to Jimmy. "Pull a stroke now" — "Back her a couple" — "Pull easy, easy" — "Back half a stroke" — and so on. This called for no particular comment. I knew that Jamesie had fished the lake for fifty years, and had an eye on him like a travelling rat. All parts of the shallow sliding past under the keel might look equally enticing to me, one part of the bay as good as another, but to his observation, backed by experience and a most remarkable memory, there might be a significant difference. He was always recalling past victories. "Twenty throut did I get to my own rod on the shore of that island in an easht wind and a shining sun, and all of them on a Grey Monkey. It was the September of the year that the ould Queen died and maybe the throut were still in half mournin'." With such a precedent, the wind east and the sun bright, what was I to do but put on a Grey

Monkey and let Jamesie control the drift? And sure enough the trout took it, even though no royalty had lately deceased.

I began to work out the effect of his orders. "Pull easy" and "Back easy" kept the boat working diagonally to left or right across the natural line of drift, and were explicable on the assumption that there was an underwater bank running obliquely to that line. "Pull a stroke" and "Back a stroke" or "Pull two" and "Back two" shifted the boat two or four lengths to right or left of the line she was on and set a new drift parallel to, but some distance from, the old. Each of these manoeuvres gave both rods fresh water, no doubt, in Jamesie's judgment, better water. But what about "Back half a stroke" or "Pull half a stroke"? The result of the first was to allow Jamesie to fish the line I had been fishing, and of the second to put me on Jamesie's line and give him new water. I became suspicious that Jamesie would not take my line, or give me his, unless he thought the change was to his advantage.

On the morning of the third day a trout took a daddy directly down wind of me and about forty yards away. If the boat were left to her natural drift I was bound to fish the spot where the trout had risen; but when we had gone about twenty yards there came the order for which I was waiting. "Back half a stroke." It was time for me to act. "Do no such thing, Jimmy," I said "If anyone is going to fish that trout it will be me and not Jamesie."

The effect of my remark on Jimmy was startling. For two days he had been following directions, comprehending perfectly that Jamesie was trying to get the better of me, amused and yet a little disapproving, for he was naturally loyal to his employer. Still, it was none of his business to interfere. Let me find out for myself if I was able. Now that I had found out he was free to enjoy the biting of the biter. He shipped both oars carefully, put his two hands on his knees, and laughed out to the heavens. "Begob, Jamesie, you're losht. The gentleman has ye discovered." Jamesie looked at us both with dignity, and then delivered a rebuke addressed to Jimmy but aimed at me. "Ye should know by this, Jimmy McDonagh, that that was a thravellin' throut and wherever he is now he is not where he rose lasht."

Jamesie had saved his face but he had been warned. "Pull half a stroke" and "Back her half" ceased to figure in his instructions. He still held the trumps. He knew the lake and I did not. If he said "Pull two strokes," or gave any command which gave both rods a new line, I was helpless. Automatically to halve his order might do us both harm, and anyhow Jamesie would have been quick enough to counter by directing the boat to be moved twice the distance he wanted. I felt sure I was being foxed and could not prove it. I tried bluff. "Look here, Jamesie, either you play fair or there will be only one rod fishing in this boat." Jamesie looked at me. His moustache moved. His eyes creased. Then he in his turn broke into laughter. He had had his fun, and it was time to stop. "Very well Sir. I'll play fair." And play fair — or very nearly fair — he did from that on.

T H Kingsmill Moore, *A Man May Fish*

FISHERMEN'S TALES

CHAPTER 3

Are anglers liars — or do they merely exaggerate? Wherever the truth, the legend, myth or calumny remains as a popular refutation of the angler's veracity.

Small wonder too, when one considers what follows in this chapter of unlikelihoods and even untruths. Here is R Allen's wonderful Major capturing a hare and a salmon at the one time, following this by landing a 33-pound trout and capping it all by riding a salmon ashore! Splendid stuff!

But there are other tales too — Luard's spooky experience on the Awbeg, Colonel Cane's fastidiously particular salmon, the bird that caught the fish, the tinker's timely deliverance in Maxwell's 'Wild Sports of the West', A A Luce's lost and found Red Spinner, and the collapse of the General. Diverse they are, but they have in common the lengths to which anglers will go to entertain and amuse — and aye, to deceive.

Mr. Pat. Lysaght, a tolerable angler, and a sporting character named Luke Morony, were fishing Tedane before dinner, and each had killed a very large trout. The two fish were so nearly equal in length and breadth, that the most practised eye could scarcely perceive a difference. A bet of a crown or two dozen of flies was made as to which was the heavier. On coming to dinner they were weighed; when, to the astonishment of Mr. Lysaght and all beholders, Luke's trout weighed a half-pound more than Mr. Lysaght's.

"Why," exclaimed he, ejaculating a round oath, — "is not this most extraordinary? Surely no one could suppose that there could be more than an ounce or so between them at most; yet see here!" taking his trout by the tail, and shaking him — when lo, a large stable key protruded from his mouth! At this, as may be supposed, there was a general laugh.

"Be not surprised, sir," quoth Luke, also taking his trout in the same way, and shaking him well; when there issued, one by one, from his gullet, thirteen large bullets! — Luke had been shooting seals on the sea-coast. The laugh was now universal, and the bystanders adjudged that the bet was fairly won by Luke, and it was accordingly paid. How Izaac Walton would have been startled by an occurrence of this kind!

O'Gorman, *The Practice of Angling*

THE HARE AND THE SALMON

R. Allen, otherwise 'Cosmopolite', wrote what are rightly held to be the most outrageous lies about Irish angling, its fish, their size and quantity. This is a good example of his mendacious mind.

"Hear the major," says the priest; "he'll tell the story."

"By the sowl of me, and I'll tell it any how."

"Tell it right, major."

"Is there a man would say that to me but your own good-looking self, now, Father?"

I begged to hear the story.

"You *must* believe it," said the priest.

"And who doesn't?" said the major, gulping down his third tumbler of punch, and slamming the glass on the table. Then, turning to me — "Sir, everybody knows the fact — I caught a hare and a salmon at one cast of the fly!"

"Oh, Benedicite," says the priest.

"None of your holy bother, now, Father. I'm after relating to the gentleman this remarkable adventure. Give me the matarials."

The needful was soon prepared; and the major, directing his conversation exclusively to me, proceeded to say that, while fishing in the Lee, not far from Macroom, he saw a fine fish rise under the opposite bank. He immediately drew out his line, so as to enable him by a cast to reach the exact spot. He had previously put on two large flies, such as are commonly used for salmon in high water. He drew back the line which would extend thirty or forty yards behind him. On endeavouring to make the cast, he found he had, as fishermen call it, "hitched behind". At this moment the salmon rose again in the same spot, and, in his eagerness to cover him, he gave a strenuous jerk, with the intent of breaking one fly, and covering the salmon with the other. Splash into the river went something heavy, which immediately took to swimming towards the opposite bank, close to the spot where the salmon had risen. The action of the animal so effectually played the other fly before the salmon, that he forthwith seized it, and both were well hooked. The major continued to relate that hereupon commenced a hard struggle; sometimes the salmon was on the surface, and sometimes the other was drawn under water, till, by judicious management, both were safely landed, and proved to be a fine hare, hooked by the leg, and a salmon of twenty pounds weight!

R Allen, *The Sportsman in Ireland*

THE BITER BIT

As an example of the daring determination of the poachers of this out-of-the-way district, it may be related that some years ago, when the tacksman, who since the opening of that particular season had hardly had a fish in his nets, happened to be at the mouth of the Bunowen on one Sunday morning, and, seeing a few fish splashing in the sea, he persuaded his men to shoot the net, which when brought to the shore, to his great joy, held more than one hundred splendid silvery fellows. Thinking that he had done sufficient law-breaking for one day, and delighted with the result, he had the nets hung up to dry, while resolving to be hard at work again early the next day.

On coming to the river on Monday morning he found that his nets had vanished during the night, while, maddening to behold, the fish were pushing their way up the river in hundreds. Now, the poachers of the district had heard of the Sunday great haul, so, fearing that the tacksman would get every fish, they stole his nets, which as long as the run lasted they kept possession of, while poaching the river every night and making large takes. As soon as the run was over the missing property was returned to the poles it had been removed from! In this case, perhaps, the tacksman was as bad as the poachers; nevertheless, our sympathies have always been with him, although probably enlisted on his side by hearing a friend relate the story in the terse, strong language in which it was told to him by the unfortunate victim.

Augustus Grimble, *The Salmon Rivers of Ireland*

The location is the River Lee in County Cork — and a delightful if apocryphal tale this is too.

"Haven't I seen them weeshty bits of pinkeens take a fly as big as thimselves clane off the very nose of a fish, and him after rising grand. Sure it's the very divil they are, and if it wasn't for thim wans coming back from the sea as grand fish, it's better out of the river they'd be. When I was a lad now, we'd be catching pinkeens all the time and niver a word from a soul. Why now, my old grandma, wouldn't she be sending me down to the river to catch thim, herself being fond of a mess of fish, and divil a care did she care if they was 'brickeens' or 'pinkeens.'

"'Paddy,' she sez, 'there's yer Uncle Tim coming to supper.'

"'I know,' sez I.

"'Paddy,' sez she, 'ye have yer little rod.'

"'I know,' sez I.

"'Well, off with you now to the river, and don't you be after coming back without a dishful, or I'll be belting the hide off you.'

"Well, away I went to the river with a bite of bread to be easing the hunger, and by evening time I had a couple of dozen of the nicest little fellers that ever ye saw. I was just thinking I had enough for the old lady, and was dragging in a small wan, when bang, swish, the biggest pike that ever ye saw had him off the hook and away with him. 'Well now,' sez I, 'did ye ever see the like of that now? But I'll have ye yet, me foine feller, an' ye taking the bread out o' me mouth.' So off I goes upstream and rigs up a wire trace and a couple of triangles, with a fine lively pinkeen just caught by the lip and the back fin to thim, and I floats him downstream to that ould divil, kicking and struggling.

"Up he came to it again, wumph, but divil a bite did he get of it this time, thim hooks having him caught grand. It took some time for me to be landing him with the little rod, and whin I had him cauld, didn't I have to belt him up the stones with my fut, and him barking and snapping with the big teeth of him like O'Hinnisey's 'Shep,' me being feared to handle him at all. Well now, I caught him a lick or two on the back of his head with a stone, and slid him into the bag along with the pinkeens, and off I goes home as proud as Mother Moriarty on market day, and her with a sup taken.'

"Whin I gets up to the house, I slips in through the back door and hangs up the bag where the cat will not be getting at it, and me thinking to hear a screech from herself whin she comes to lift it down, and off I goes to meet the uncle in the bohareen beyant.

"Whin we gets back, and he and his ma had done colloguing, she says to me: 'Were you after bringing back thim pinkeens?'

"'I was so,' sez I, with a wink at me uncle.

"'And where may they be?' sez herself.

"'Hanging behint the door,' sez I, and away she goes to cook the supper.

"Well now, I grabs me uncle by the arm and whispers to him to come and hear the fun, but just as we gets to the door the cat comes out screeching and spitting like the Ould Wan himself, and the grandma starts yellin' and bawlin' like the Last Day of Judgment, and whin we gets in, there was herself on the table and the ould divil of a pike hoppin' and snappin' round the floor as lively as a kitten.

"Well, the uncle grabs the chopper and fetches that wan a skelp and has him laid out quiet, and thin the ould lady says:

"'What for are ye bringing home that divil for? And me asking for pinkeens.'

"'They're in the bag with him,' sez I.

"'They are not,' sez she. 'There's divil a thing else but that wan that came leppin' and roarin' out at me like the O'Flaherty's bull.'

"'What?' sez I. 'There's twenty-eight of as grand pinkeens as iver came out of the river.'

"'Ye're lying,' sez she. 'And ye wasting your time catching that thing that ain't fit to be feeding to the bonhams.' And with that herself starts reaching for the ash-plant she always kept in the corner.

" 'Hould on a bit, ma,' sez me Uncle Tim. 'How many did ye say ye had caught?'

" 'Twinty-eight of thim,' sez I, starting to blubber, me knowing well I had thim wans caught, and fearing a belting. 'The cat must have had thim ate on me.'

" 'Divil a cat would have got in that bag,' sez herself. 'That wan with thim teeth would have had any cat ate before it got its head inside the bag.' And she starts reaching for the ash-plant again.

" 'Hould on,' sez me uncle again. 'Maybe ye're right now.'

"And with that he grabs the knife and slits that ould divil down the belly, and out comes the pinkeens, slithering and slopping all over the floor. That ould scamer had them swallered, and he in the bag with them.

"Well, I must be going now, I see himself below there has met with a fish."

And I was left gasping, like a freshly caught trout, on the bank.

W Durand, *Wanderings with a fly-rod*

"Hould on," cried Owen, in the midst of our apostrophes; "he's here, your honour." He had hooked a fine fish on the flat.

"Faith and there's corn still in Egypt," exclaimed the major; "where the deuce is my fly-book?"

He was soon prepared, and as soon rose a salmon — another — he is hooked.

"The landing-net," cried Owen.

"The landing-net," cried the major.

I stood between the two combatants, knowing not which to assist.

"The gaff," cries the major; "let the spalpeen hould on."

At that moment a magnificent fish leapt from the water — down went the major's rod — "and that's a fair one, any way," said the major; "he'll give us a run, yet. A hand for the saints."

I assisted him to disencumber himself of his coat and hat. "Now we start fair" — but the fish was lodged; it was the largest salmon I had seen, and I confess I shared all the sportsman's anxiety with the major. "Off again" — he was off, indeed; and it was impossible to follow, so ludicrous a figure did the major present, puffing down the stream, utterly unable to guide his steps, his whole attention being on the reel which was running at a fearful rate, notwithstanding his own exertions to follow the fish.

"Gone, by St. Patrick!" exclaimed the major, dashing the rod into the stream, and falling squat into a bog on his face. I hastened to his assistance; and Owen, having landed his fish, was before me. We raised the major in anxiety — he scraped the mud from his eyes and mouth, and, as quickly as he could, exclaimed, "Never mind me; follow the fish — I'm done — " and, in a pathetic but earnest manner, made out in signs what the masses of mud in his mouth would by no means allow him to utter.

We were both sportsmen too well seasoned to hesitate; but the rod was gone, and a long run we had to overtake it. There it was, in the middle of the stream — nothing but the top to be seen, the weight of the reel sinking the but; and, to our mortification, a slack line.

"That's a misfortune, any way," said Owen; "the fish is gone."

"Gone!" cried the major, who now came up, and who had by this time so well effected the process of cleansing by his pocket handkerchief, that he had succeeded in well covering every part of his face, hair, hands, and clothes, with the brown bog mud — he looked like an animated masterpiece of Vandyke.

"Give me your rod" — with a dexterous cast he covered the top, and caught the line with the flies of Owen's apparatus — "gently, and don't disturb him if he's there." It was a moment of real suspense — the rod was recovered — the line reeled in, which had at least one hundred yards out. It was now found to have taken a different course, and the fish had again turned up the stream — the line was fixed.

"He's here," cried the major.

"Huzza!" exclaimed Owen, in extreme delight; "this is a fishing!"

"Now, major, for your skill — if you lose that fish — "

"Be aisy," said the major, "the time's against me — he has not been idle all this time — he has been busy enough grubbing at the bottom, to get the hook out of his mouth — faith and he'll give us another leap yet."

As he approached the spot where the fish was sulkily ensconced, I could perceive the paleness of the cheek — the quivering of the lip — both so indicative of extreme excitement, that I began to question my own nerve. I was not much more calm — this was a prize. The major did not venture to hint at the weight, but it was obvious that he felt he had an enemy worthy of his utmost skill.

The fish now gradually and gently moved up the stream; a steady but tight strain was kept on the line, which the reel gradually received, giving token of an approach to the surface. He came, like a log of wood, to the top. A fish, indeed — for one minute I had a perfect view of him as he broke the water with an enormous tail.

The major grew still more nervous; yet the steadiness with which he held the rod was admirable. "Beware now," says he. Up went the fish, at least five yards into the air! — the rod was again down, and recovered at the moment of the splash occasioned by his fall. "He's safe," whispered the veteran — "that last spring has tired him." He struggled with some violence for some minutes — I was ready with the gaff — he came gently to the shore, turned two or three times on his stomach, and I plunged the hook into his side.

It was well that I did so at that moment — the fly had worn out of his mouth, and he was free from the line. "Huzza!" cried Owen and the major, in which I heartily joined — up went our hats, in token of our triumph — the monster floundered on the shore.

"Salmon," cries the major — "the devil a salmon at all!"

It was, indeed, no salmon, but one of the great Lake trout, the largest that had been seen for many years, even from the broad waters of Lough Corrib. Its weight exceeded thirty-three pounds. The memory of this fish has not passed away — it may still be heard of among the cottagers, many of whom saw it.

R Allen, *The Sportsman in Ireland*

"I remember now wan of the strangest flies I ever tied to be catching a fish with; and it did so, though by the same token I niver did be tying it at all, at all, except to me hook. I was only a ladeen at the time and was doing gillie to the ould earl. Herself was wanting a salmon for the gintry at dinner that night, and himself was away at the Parliament House in England, and *that* at the start of the fishing season! So I took me rod down to the river, and well I remimber I was fishing downstream for three hours without meeting with a fish.

"Well, now, I knew that Mary, the cook above there at the castle, would be roarin' and bawlin' if so be I was late with the fish, and it's worried I was getting that I could not meet with one. I was wading in the shallows at the head of the 'Blue Hole' when I saw a fish boil at the tail of it, just where the water breaks, and where the branch of a tree leans over the water, and at the same time a pair of blackbirds starts yellin' and shriekin' like Bridie Malone, and her with the high strikes.

" 'Phwat the divil's all that?' sez I, and I goes down there to see.

"Well now, I'll be telling you, wasn't there a bird's nest right out on the end of that branch, and weren't the young birds crawling and squaking on the edge of it, and thim with just a fluffeen of feathers to their backs, and the ould birds swooping down to the water and bawling blue murther. 'Hah,' sez I, 'hasn't one of thim wans fallen in and a pike had him cot at once, it was never a salmon I saw at all.'

"But as I was standing there, didn't a salmon, as big as a calf, roll over in the water just below me.

" 'Well,' sez I, 'if it's young birds ye be wanting, don't I know of a frosted nest of dead wans ye can have with all the joy in the world.' And I drops me rod and goes tearing back to the garden as fast as the Divil himself, and I comes back with two three dead birds in me hat, and whips one of thim same on to me hook before you could be shpitting in the water.

" 'Now, me foine lad,' sez I, 'let's be seeing if it's still hungry ye are.' And with that I flops the young bird on the water where the stream will just be catching it.

"Up that fish comes with a 'Wumph' and I drives the hook home in him, me roarin' and bawlin' so Dan Meggarty above there on the road would be hearing, and him the darlin' man with the gaff. Dan comes rowling down the hill, spacheless with the haste of him, thinking maybe that it's drownding in the river I was.

" 'Have ye hoult of the Ould Wan himself?' sez he.

" 'I have so,' sez I, and with that the scamer leps six feet clear of the water and starts for the sea with his back fin out.

" 'Hould him tight,' sez Dan, running down the bank after me.

" 'And how would I be houlding him tighter,' sez I, 'and him tearing the line out, and me lepping like a goat to be kaping with him at all.'

"Well now, he turns at Sir George's rock, and it's more than an hour it's fighting him I was before Dan can get the hook in him.

" 'And that's the biggest fish that ever came out of the Lee,' sez Dan, and him sthruggling up the bank with it.

" 'It is so,' sez I.

" 'And phwat fly did ye have him cot with at all?' sez Dan.

" 'Oh, just wan of me own tying,' sez I , hoping Dan would not be looking too close; but with that he opens the fish's mouth, and belave me or belave me not, there was the hook, fast in his jaw, as bare as the back of your hand.

" 'Well now,' sez he, 'and that's the strange sort of fly to be using at all.'

" 'Ah,' sez I, 'he has the feathers ate off of it, and him leppin' and kickin' like Mother Moriarty's ass.' And I turns over me hat with a skelp of me fut so Dan would not be seeing thim other young birdeens.

" 'It's a poor fly ye'll be tying that has the feathers ate off it so soon.'

" 'Maybe so, but it has the fish cot that herself does be wanting above there in the castle.' And with that I humps it on my back and starts out for the kitchen, and when Mary comes to be cleaning that wan, divil the sign of a bird was there in its stomach. Will ye be telling me now, why was that fish taking thim two birds and not to be swallerin' thim at all? It has me bate entirely.

W Durand, *Wanderings with a fly-rod*

One more tale and I must say farewell to the Liffey. Another officer, also a rival, had agreed with me that a day's trouting near the famous bridge was desirable from every point of view. But at the last moment I was delayed by some wretched orderly-corporal or something, and he went on ahead. I fished after him to the lodge gates, but caught nothing. Going inside to leave my rod, I saw his bag, a peep into which revealed five brace of most excellent trout. To transfer them to my own and fill his up with stones delayed me but a few minutes more, and very soon I reached the house, where they were all going into lunch. Her Ladyship asked after my sport, and I begged her acceptance of my catch, which I proudly turned out on the lawn. "Oh! how splendid!" said her eldest daughter. "What a fisherman you are." I glanced at my rival. "Indeed," said he, "I have just as many down at the lodge. I hope you will accept mine too." But this they said they could not consent to, and as we biked back in the cool of the evening my comrade complained bitterly of the weight of his bag. Next morning he told his servant to have a trout done for my breakfast and one for his own, and he'd find them in his bag in the next room. "Will ye have them broiled or fried, sorr?" asked his man a minute later, producing a handful of stones to his astonished gaze. Oh! Bard of Athy! You are not often sold, but you were done very brown that time, my boy, and you know it, though you did try so manfully to brazen it out. Very pleasant were those days beside the beautiful Liffey, albeit the fish were few and far between, and most of us suffered dreadfully from midge bites.

A Mainwaring, *Fishing and Philandering*

George Burrows was angling correspondent of The Irish Times *for many years, while Des Elliott is a Dublin angler who has probably caught more double-figure brown trout than any living Irish angler.*

Two splendid angling stories have been told to me by Des Elliott, a Dublin angler known to many of us. So this week I hand over this feature temporarily to him. The account he gives is well worth remembering, indeed filing away.

He writes: "Two tales of big trout on Lough Mask which may be of interest. Wednesday, 8th September. There are four of us in two boats, myself and my friend, his daughter and his brother-in-law. We take an early lunch as the breeze, which was good on setting out from Cushlough, has died away and there is no sign of it returning.

"We have fly rods and dapping rods, but no spinning rods for trolling. I do have a small box of baits in my jacket pocket and we rig up the dapping rods by removing the floss lines and attaching baits to the backing. My friend's daughter comes with me in my boat. I have rigged up her rod with a No. 5 Mepps.

"It occurs to me that this rod is too soft to set a large treble hook trailed 50 yards behind the boat but it will have to do.

"Three hundred yards after leaving the island we pass over a shallow. I say to her that the bait is sure to get hung up here. Sure enough, just after passing over it the rod doubles over. I tell her to pick up the rod and wind in while I turn the boat and go back to retrieve the bait. She winds in the line while I slowly drive the boat back.

"It never occurs to me that it is anything other than the bottom that the bait is attached to. When we are about 20 yards from where the line enters the water she says to me that she thinks there is a fish on the end of the line. I say it can't be, it is the bottom. I stand up to have a look, just in case. In front of the boat, under the surface I see a long grey shape with a huge white mouth. I say to her that you have a pike of about 12-14 lb and I sit down thinking that there will be some fun playing this lad.

"The fish moves around a quarter circle clockwise till it is opposite the side of the boat and then rolls on the surface. We see the whole fish. It is a trout — it is a huge trout! The fish heads back in the direction it had come. She gets nervous and won't play the fish. I take the rod. The fish makes a long run. I gain line on it. The fish starts boring and makes short runs. The fish comes alongside the boat, but it is too deep to see. The line is vertical in the water. Suddenly it feels slack. I reel in just with a feeling of panic. It does not tighten again. The bait breaks the surface — the great fish has gone. The fish was around 18 lb — the biggest trout I have ever seen.

"In Art O'Neill's bar (in Ballinrobe) that night we compare the length of the fish that we saw in the lake that afternoon with one in a glass case over the bar. This fish weighs 12½ lb. We agree that it was about half as long again. What a trout!

"Wednesday, 22nd September. Exactly two weeks later I set out from Cushlough at about 1 p.m. At the same time young Eamonn Sheridan of Cushlough goes out fishing with a German visitor. At around 4 p.m. I see this boat about 400 yards away from me. The two of them are standing up in the boat, with rods in the air. I think to myself they must have got their lines crossed and I continue fishing.

"About 15 minutes later I look over at them again and they are still standing up in the boat with rods raised. Then I see a landing net lowered and a large fish brought into the boat. I thought the fish would be about 7 lb weight, judging from the distance I was away from them.

"Even though the fish has been landed they still continue to stand up in the boat. I could not figure out what was going on. Then I realised that they must have two big lads on at the same time.

"I start the engine and go towards them. As I approach I see the landing net produced again and a much larger fish is landed.

When I draw alongside their boat I see on the boards two very big trout thrashing about.

"The two fish had been hooked at *exactly the same time*. The weights were 13 lb 10 oz and 8 lb 8 oz. The bigger fish took a No. 3 Mepps and the smaller a 2-inch blue and silver Devon. A magnificent brace of trout and a remarkable angling achievement. They were the only fish they caught that day."

A splendid angling story — and thank you very much, Des.

George Burrows, *The Irish Times*, October, 1982

Colonel Cane, who was a keen fisherman and an artist with the prawn, told me a salmon story which I should not have believed from anyone else. He said that one day when the water was low he was sitting above the fall and saw two fish lying below him. He threw his prawn above them and beside them, time after time, and they paid no attention. Finally he put it in front of one of the fish and let it lie there. Then the salmon slowly approached it, lifted it with the edge of its lips, swam with it to an adjacent flat rock just covered with water, left it there, and swam back to its original position. Colonel Cane's theory was that it was just bored with the perpetual reappearance of the prawn, and wished to remove the annoyance as soon as it could be done without danger. I wonder.

Maurice Headlam, *Irish Reminiscences*

Then the Chairman intervened and called on me to continue, which I did more or less as follows:

"I also have had one curious experience," I said, 'Only the other day, when salmon fishing with a friend in Ireland, we saw a nice fish rising in an easy flowing flat. My friend hooked this fish at his first cast and eventually brought him into the bank for me to gaff. This I duly did. "All right: I've got him", I said "but the fly is out of his mouth". "No you haven't", he cried, and looking up I saw that his rod was still bent in a curve. The salmon I had gaffed, was, as they sometimes do, one which had followed his hooked companion to see what was going on. We got them both.'

G D Luard, *Fishing Fact or Fantasy*

I will here relate a curious adventure which took place on the river Donbeg or Cooraclare, an excellent salmon river, but very foul and full of stumps. I had lost so many flies and salmon by these stumps that I determined on cross fishing it, and I got a tolerable angler in my neighbourhood to accompany me.

We have a strong five-fly cross line, with silk line droppers, and our flies on all good three-gut; and came on an excellent reach, with a fine breeze against the current, which was slight. We had only just commenced, when a large flock of tame geese flew very swiftly over the river, and in a direct line with our cross line. We most unfortunately raised our hands, and instantly had three of them firm.

It is almost impossible to describe the scene — splashing, swimming, flying, running up and down the river for nearly an hour; and, to complete our confusion, at my companion's side, a set of outrageous women, hearing the noise and outcry, came down, and if they could have got stones, would have annihilated him, charging him as the cause of the state their geese were in. At length he was forced to run for his life, having cut the line and the concern at once. At length (but not until the geese were nearly dead) I contrived to land the line, and with great difficulty extracted the flies. The reach was destroyed, my companion had fled, the wind fell away, and I walked disconsolately to the village of Cooraclare, about a mile distant, where I was glad to take some rest after the great fatigue and vexation I had undergone.

O'Gorman, *The Practice of Angling*

"Extent! is it extent you mane? Look ye, sir — I am a Major in his Majesty's army, and am paid by a rascally government: and, sir, I have never lost my character for veracity. Extent! — by the honour of the commission I hold, I once rode a salmon astride out of the stream, and spurred him ashore!"

A burst of surprise and admiration, from those least acquainted with the major, followed this assertion.

"Rode a salmon ashore? Impossible!" says the priest.

"Verum quia impossibile, I presume you mean," said I; "the major will explain."

"Troth and I will, and the devil help the spalpeen that is not satisfied with it. I repeat again, I rode a salmon astride, and spurred him ashore. — Father, you know the shallows leading to the mill of Ballyvourneen."

"A good spot for a salmon," says the priest, "but bad for riding him."

"You shall hear — I had been to Ballyvourneen, and was returning to Macroom, on horseback, in the evening. I had had a long ride. Where the road passes by the side of the river, and along the shallow which falls into the *good people's hole,* whom should I see, hard at work with a salmon, but Phelim, the piper. Hold on there, says I — and, booted and spurred as I was, I dashed into the stream, and seized the rod from the piper, who never had a steady hand, and was timid. The salmon was in the hole, above which I stood in the shallows, and about mid-stream. The moment the fish moved, I knew his weight to be above forty pounds, for it's meself can tell to an ounce the weight of a fish at the first plunge. Away went the salmon, and away went the reel. I held on firmly and tightly till the line was nearly out; when, all at once, the fresh run fish dashed up the stream. I reeled away as quick as lightning, lest I should lose my hold; and, as the stream was strong, I bent my knees in the water to get a firmer hold on my legs, and to give me the power of winding quick. Suddenly

I felt myself lifted off my legs! Oh, Bubbaboo, says I — it was but an instant — Is an Irishman ever at a loss? — I caught hold of the line for a bridle, stuck my spurs into the side of the fish, which I now found closely stuck between my legs, and with one bound we were both in the high shallows, where I safely landed the monster, to the immortal honour of fishing and the excellent dinner of Lord V_____, who swore if any other man had said he had caught him in the same way, he would not have believed him."

R Allen, *The Sportsman in Ireland*

Nevertheless, fond of it as I am, this fishing alone at night can be an eerie business, and inured as I am to it, there have been occasions when I should have found it pleasanter — I might even say reassuring — to have had a companion.

One such I remember years ago, when I was about seventeen. I had set out alone to fish the Grove, a gloomy length of the Little River, a long way below the house, where the trout are big and there are many trees.

The trout were inclined to take, but it was exceptionally dark, trees and bushes took on strange shapes in the obscurity, and gradually a sense of uneasiness began to steal over me.

I did my best to throw it off — told myself it was nonsense. But it was no use — the feeling only intensified.

It was extraordinarily still. I began to listen, a fatal thing to do, but all I could hear was the tinkling of the nearby river, and the surreptitious rustlings of small creatures in the grass.

The atmosphere was definitely evil, and suddenly my childish nightmare days seemed to grip me and I began to feel that at any moment I might be confronted with some amorphous horror. Then my nerve gave way and I fled, as if the devil was after me, as perhaps he was. Roots tripped me and brambles tore my clothes as I hurried home through the pitchy blackness. How my rod escaped damage I do not know, but not until I had entered the big sleeping house and turned on the lights did ease of mind return. I have experienced other eerie moments, as most sensitive people have, but never with such intensity or with such a sense of surrounding malignity. Possibly if I had had the sagacious Jock as my companion, I should not have felt so alone and helpless.

Next morning I met Tom Lonergan scuffling the drive and laughingly told him of my experience. He took it perfectly seriously. After ruminating a moment with his eyes on the ground — he looked up and said, 'Tis a bad place altogether; ten thousand asses wouldn't drag me there at night for all the fish in Ireland.'

He then told me the following tale, which I reproduce as nearly in his style as I can remember.

'It's a long time now there was an old woman lived in Grove House.' This the farm just outside the front gates of Ballyhimmock, and a little above the spot where I had been fishing the night before. 'It was she was a queer one. Wasn't it unnatural the way she lived to herself entirely and hardly crossed her own doorsteps, and she with plenty to live on and nothing to show for it at all.

'Well, in the end she died — a great age she was — and what did she leave? Only an ass nearly as old as herself and a few pounds tied up in a dirty handkerchief. That couldn't be all there was anyway — an old miser, that's what she was of course, and somewhere or other in the house she had her treasure hid, and little good it had done the old witch — God rest her!

'That was what the village said. Be damn, there was treasure too — and as the place was empty the half of the men would be going there one time and another to look for the treasure — in the day I mean, for not one of them would venture there in the dark, and I wouldn't blame them. They searched the house from the roof to the cellar, and from cellar to roof; they dug up the potato patch and garden — divil a one of them had ever worked so hard in their lives. 'Twas all one, not a penny did they find, and the end of it was they got tired and gave it up.

'But there was one young fellow — and a bad one at that — he was not so young either — and he had an idea where the treasure might be.

'He was a mean sort of a man, the kind that wouldn't share a crust with his own mother. Well, one night off he goes to the house in the dead of the dark to search, and I wouldn't say but what he had drink taken to keep up his courage. It would be about midnight two young men at the top of the village saw him pass running like mad and he panting, "The old woman's after me — the old woman's after me" — and with that he dashed in at his own door, which was near, and fell down dead. Faith, there's some says the old woman walks yet.'

Tom Lonergan shifted the weight of his lean body on the handle of the scuffle and a fleeting smile passed over his face and disappeared as he added: 'I wouldn't say but what he had drink taken — but anyway 'tis a bad place.'

Superstition dies hard in Ireland, and in these days of over-rationalization — horrible word — when the masses with their misapplied smattering of science believe that the only miracles are in the hands of man — perhaps it is no bad thing.

G D Luard, *Fishing Fortunes and Misfortunes*

William Hamilton Maxwell's Wild Sports of the West *is the single best-known Irish sporting book, an enduring classic with its poignant reminders of a sporting era long vanished in the wild west of Mayo.*

"The best practical lesson I ever got originated in the following accidental occurrence. Some years ago I received private information, that a travelling tinker, who occasionally visited these mountains to make and repair the tin stills used by the peasantry in illicit distillation, was in the constant habit of destroying fish, and he was represented as being a most successful poacher. I was returning down the river after an unfavourable day, a wearied and a disappointed fisherman, and observed, at a short distance, a man chased across the bogs by several others, and eventually overtaken and secured. It was the unfortunate tinker, surprised by the keepers in the very act of landing a splendid salmon; two, recently killed, were discovered in his wallet, and yet that blessed day I could not hook a fish! He was forthwith brought in durance before *my honour,* to undergo the pains and penalties of his crime. He was a strange, raw-boned, wild-looking animal, and I half suspect Sir Walter Scott had seen him before he sketched Watt Tinlin in the 'Lay'. He was a convicted felon — he had no plea to offer, for he was taken in the very fact. But he made two propositions wherewithal to obtain his liberty — 'He would never sin again — or he would fight any two of the captors.' My heart yearned towards him — he was after all a brother — and admitting that rod and coat were not worth threepence, still he was an adept in the 'gentle art,' although the most ragged disciple that ever Walton boasted. I forgave him, dismissed the captors, and ordered him to the Lodge for refreshment. 'My honour had no sport,' and he looked carelessly at my flies. 'Would I condescend to try one of his?' and he put a strange-looking combination of wool and feathers on the casting-line. There was a fine pool near us — I tried it, and at the second cast I was fast in a twelve-pound salmon! My ragged friend remained with me some days; and in his sober intervals, 'few and far between,' gave me lessons in the art, that have been more serviceable than any I had hitherto acquired.

"Two years after, I was obliged to attend the winter fair of Ball to purchase cattle. It was twilight when I left it, and I had proceeded only a few miles towards a gentleman's house, where I was to dine and sleep, when my horse cast a shoe, and forced me to leave him at a smith's shop, which was fortunately at hand. The evening was chilly, and I determined to proceed on foot, directing my servant to follow. I passed a lonely *poteen-house* — several ruffian-looking fellows were on the road beside it. They were half-drunk and insolent — I was rash — words borrowed blows, and I soon discovered that I should have the worst of the battle, and was tolerably certain of a sound drubbing. Suddenly, an unexpected ally came to my assistance; he *dropped* the most formidable of the assailants as if he had been struck down by a sledge-hammer. A few blows settled the contest; and I turned round to recognise and thank my deliverer. ''Pon my sowl, you're mighty handy, Master Julius; it's a murder that ye don't practise oftener!' The speaker was my gifted friend — the tinker."

W H Maxwell, *Wild Sports of the West*

I was fishing from a boat on the Upper Reservoir at Bohernabreena, a few miles from Dublin, with my friend, Mr. Bindon Scott, a solicitor, now with God. In those days the Rathmines Town Council was in being, and controlled the fishing and performed the functions that now come under the Dublin Corporation. I had three small flies on my cast — my pet Red Spinner on the bob, a Silver Priest on the tail, and what the middle dropper was I forget, and it is of no account. There was no nylon then; we fished gut and nothing but gut. Gut in *some* respects, not *all*, was better than nylon; but gut needed soaking, and if worked or knotted dry, it would crack or draw and weaken; in consequence breaks occurred often. Moreover the trout were gut-shy, and we fished fine. I was casting from the stern of the boat; my Red Spinner was bobbing attractively in the surface ruffle; a fish rose; there was a short, sharp jerk, and nothing more happened. It was a break. Most anglers have known that anguish. The fish had broken the fly from the cast. Presumably he broke it with his mouth; but sometimes they lash out at the fly with fin or tail. In such cases the fly is usually left sticking in the fish, and he goes off to the rubbing stump, or engages the help of the tench, reputed the doctor-fish.

Nothing like that occurred in this case. That trout broke my Red Spinner somehow from the cast; but he did not go off with it in mouth or fin or tail. Neither I nor (so far as I know) any other angler met that trout again; yet the fly he broke off is back in my fly-box. That clever trout somehow managed to break my Red Spinner from its gut-point, and spit it out or otherwise get rid of it instantaneously. How he did so I cannot imagine; but he did so; it was a strange happening.

A stranger happening was to follow. I recovered my fly against all the chances in a scarcely credible way. I tell it in the words I wrote in the correspondence columns of *The Irish Angler*, Summer Number, 1939.

"We were in deep water; by all the chances that fly, falling from the fish's mouth, should have sunk to rest and rust at the bottom of the lake. But no; fate and the long arm of coincidence willed otherwise; for as I, slowly and sadly, drew the cast back into the boat for repairs, first the bob-point, flyless, then the middle dropper, and the Priest on the tail — when the silver tail-fly came up over the edge of the boat, to my amazement there, caught and safely held, hook in hook, was my lost Red Spinner."

A A Luce, *Fishing and Thinking*

From the first there was friendly rivalry between us. The General, as the doyen of the party, had many interesting experiences to tell to anyone with time to listen to them. The trouble was to get him to stop. "Luck be d_____d", he would say, "catching fish is a matter of skill and skill is the outcome of experience. What the younger generation is suffering from is too much luxury. Damme, sir, they want to be bottle-fed. Now you," he would continue, looking at me, "may make a fisherman in time. You're young yet."

Unquestionably he was a very fine fisherman, but constant bragging frays the stoutest nerves and soon in matters piscatorial I began to hate the General as cordially as I liked him in the ordinary way.

It was after he had caught a lovely fish of 14 lbs., and we were treated from soup to savoury with a recapitulation of the life history of that salmon, the fly that caught it, and the skill of the master hand that tied the fly, that my patience snapped. When he revived the topic before breakfast the next morning I fled incontinently lest I should forget my manners.

For a whole fortnight I longed for nothing so much as a chance to kill a fish an ounce or two beyond the specimen. Then came the eagerly awaited day, on which the General had business in Galway City, and I had the river to myself. Bright and early I reached the hotel beat to find, instead of my usual gillie, one, Larry Hogan. He seemed a genial and a knowledgeable bird, but neither his obvious acquaintance with the best lies nor my own unflagging industry could stir a fish, and we sat down to our sandwiches at mid-day with a solitary sea trout of about ½ lb. to show for the labour of the morning.

This was scarcely good enough, and Larry scratched his head. "I'm thinkin' ye cud do better at the Wall Pool," said he, "seein' the day that's in it, and the water the colour that it is." And he pointed to a bend in the river half a mile downstream. "But see here, your honour," Larry said, "ye'll never take them in that water with these flies. A shrimp is what ye'll need," and from a capacious pocket he produced a stock of prawns, and bade me carry on.

Well, believe it or not, in less than five minutes I was into a tidy fish. I will not labour the ups and downs of the encounter, suffice it to say that after as bonny a tussle as one could wish, Larry gaffed a salmon that turned the balance over 16 lb. Then I sank into the heather positively gloating over the General's discomfiture anon.

And if one salmon, why not another? So I started to work the pool again with the faithful Larry at my elbow, when a light laugh broke the silence of the afternoon, and turning I saw a girl contemplating the scene with some amusement. "Well, Larry," the damsel enquired sweetly, "up to your old tricks again?" and then she turned to me and asked, with a suspicion of a twinkle in her eye, if I knew I was trespassing. "But of course you don't," she went on, "though you have succeeded in annexing the biggest poacher in the country as your gillie."

"Sure now, Miss Nora," began Larry, "this was the way of ut_____"

But she cut him short. "You can save your breath," she said, "for you couldn't tell the truth, even by accident."

By this time I was feeling thoroughly uncomfortable, and probably looked it, for the lady began to take pity on my misery. "I suppose you are staying at the hotel," she said, "but this beat is the next one to their water, and well that old blackguard knows it. Oh! it's not the first time by a long chalk that he has persuaded a stranger to use a shrimp in this pool. No one knows better than himself that only fly fishing is allowed. But of course you aren't to blame."

Well! There was only one kind of restitution and apology I could make, and that was to render forthwith to Caesar what was most distinctly Caesar's. Besides, it struck me forcibly that even were I to return with such a handsome fish, I should be required to give chapter and verse of the exact spot and method of its capture. Then how should I get over that illicit prawn, explaining why my colleagues might not follow my example?

But at first the maid was adamant. She would not take the salmon under any consideration. She repeated that I was not a poacher by intent, that there were plenty more where it came from, and that she was sick of salmon anyway, and it was only when I hinted that my honour as a sportsman was involved that she laughed and said that in that case we might make a compromise.

"I'll tell you what," she said, "my old nurse, who lives in the cottage over yonder, has been ill, and I was going to take her some delicacies this afternoon, so I will put in the salmon as a make-weight, and if you come to tea tomorrow, my father will surely give you a day or two on the river, when, let us hope, you will get an even bigger fish!"

So with nothing but my little sea trout in the bag, I trudged slowly home. Too slowly, as it happened, to avoid a rencontre with the General, who, having returned from Galway rather ahead of expectation, had strolled out to see how I was getting on. "Any luck?" he asked. "Not much," I answered.

"Ah, my boy," he said, "what you want is more patience. You youngsters do no good because you don't know where to look for salmon in the first place, nor how to fish for them in the second." (I nearly hit him). "Why, I've just passed one of the prettiest girls I ever saw with a salmon nearly as good as the one I got the other day. Girl after my own heart, damme; rare fisherwoman she must be. Could give you some lessons, my lad."

"But," I began, now thoroughly exasperated, "that salmon was _____" and then I shut my mouth again. After all, what could I say? What could anyone have said? I could not even tell him it topped his own rotten fish by a good 2 lbs. Inwardly raging, I turned and walked beside him sadly and in silence.

J B Drought, *A Sportsman Looks at Éire*

I chummed up with a very nice English fellow called John Burberry who knew how to fish and loved the Butler Pool. The night before he was due to leave he had a small farewell party which went on into the small hours of the morning. I was about to go to bed when I was accosted by his wife saying that John was missing. She asked me to take a car down to the Butler Pool to see if he was there. They were due to take the 8 a.m. train from Cahirciveen and it was now almost 7 a.m.

I left the car on the bridge and strolled down to find John literally bent into a salmon.

'Eric. You'd hardly believe it. With my first cast I hooked him and I'm in him for the past hour.'

'I would think, John, he's foul hooked.'

'He's snagged under the far bank and I just can't get a move out of him,' he went on.

I would not be swayed and after watching the procedure for ten minutes I told him his wife was becoming very anxious as the train was leaving at 8 a.m. However, this conveyed nothing to him so I suggested getting a couple of rocks and dropping them down beside the fish. John flew at me.

'After an hour you want me to lose the biggest fish I've ever taken from the Butler Pool?' I left him alone, the train had gone. Then, really annoyed, I went to him.

'If you really want that fish let me throw a couple of bricks at him to liven him up.' By this time his arms were giving out.

'Here. You take the rod,' he said.

'No. Certainly not.' I pulled a couple of rocks from an old wall and landed them about three feet above the cast. The fish came like a tornado across the river never breaking the water and went under the near bank. A worse position than ever. By this time I had taken charge of things and I said to him,

'If you want the fish there is only one remedy. Stone him.' I brought half the wall over to the bank and slung in brick after brick. The fish took off down stream and headed for a small path on the opposite bank. Up the bank, under the wire fence and the last thing I heard was the snap of the line and the banking gone. It was the largest otter I've ever seen. I'll never forget the look on John Burberry's face. It was queer. His hands and arms were numb. All I could do was to step behind what was left of the wall and break my heart with laughter. The one that got away!

Eric Craigie, *Irish Sporting Sketches*

It was now Delaney's turn.

'Well now', he began. 'I have nothing to disbelieve in what we have heard today. It's queer things happen to us all.

'I remember once I was salmon fishing in Ireland. There were four of us on the different beats. There was a grand run of fish too, but divil a one of us could catch anything though they were jumping everywhere. Now it's a biggish river and I and my ghillie were using the boat. The cream of the fishing was just below a mill, and here they were as thick as sardines, all pushing one another and leaping at the weir. We pulled the boat up to the very top, and I had just started to fish from the tail end of it when there was a thump on the boards behind me. At the same moment the boat began to drift swiftly down stream. "What the divil are ye doing, Pat?" I called — and looking round there was Pat, who had shipped his pole, grovelling on the bottom of the boat after a nice fish of 12 lbs., which had jumped clean into the boat and was now kicking about all over the place. "By damn", said he, as he got a grip on the fish's gills, "here's one anyway that prefers dry land and I wouldn't disappoint him", and he cracked him over the head with the "priest".

'Then he picked up the pole again as if nothing had happened and pushed us back to the top again.

'I hadn't been fishing more than five minutes when "bump", another fish of 15 lbs. landed in the boat and was quickly disposed of in the same way. Would you believe it? Before we had finished, three more from 10 to 18 lbs. did exactly the same thing. You can imagine the faces of my friends when I got back to the Inn that evening with five fine salmon. They hadn't touched a fish. I may say I had taken the pains to put a hole in each of their mouths the way my friends wouldn't suspect foul play. Naturally Pat said nothing. Extraordinary that five fish should have committed suicide in this way, but Pat certainly pushed the boat up as near as he safely could to where an extraordinary number were jumping at the weir. The old villain!'

There was a groan from the assembled company and no little laughter for here was a story it would be hard to beat.

G D Luard, Fishing Fact or Fantasy

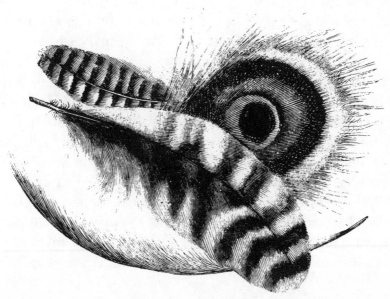

I always had a liking for Waterville, Co. Kerry. In 1928 I started to go down there twice a year with my brother Jack, once for the woodcock shooting and again for a week's fishing on Lake Currane and the Inny river. Currane is one of the prettiest lakes in Ireland; it is set at the base of the Macgillycuddy Reek mountains and joins Ballinskelligs Bay at the famous Butler Pool. Regrettably, it is too far from Dublin. We always stayed in the Butler Arms Hotel in the village, which was packed with British officers who, it appeared to me, let the gillies do the fishing and only took the rod when a fish had been hooked! In those days fishing stopped at 7 p.m. and one could not get a boat or a gillie after that hour. Thirty-five years went by before I felt I would like to take my family down there for a holiday. To my amazement I was welcomed with open arms by the staff and I was pleased to see my old boatman still hale and hearty.

At lunch one day Canon Scanlon from Dunshaughlin, Co. Meath, came to our table and asked me if I would take his son John out in the boat after dinner as he was bored stiff sitting around the hotel. Needless to say I was delighted to oblige and we arranged to meet on the pier at 7.30 p.m. I asked John if he had ever rowed or if he had any interest in fishing. His answer to the latter was a very definite no. So taking up the oars I showed him how to feather them and after a quarter of an hour's instruction John could whip the boat round onto a fish better than I have seen many an expert. We finished up by landing six brace of lovely trout. I took the leading oarsman back to the hotel with no need for further instruction and was highly delighted with our night's entertainment. I told John I had never seen a person get into the swing of using an oar as he had done.

'Well,' he said, 'you are a very good instructor but, as a matter of fact, I'm stroke for the Trinity Eight.' I nearly fell off the chair. The amateur instructing the professional how to use his oars! He was quite modest. He had never sat on a fixed seat or rowed with rollocks. We had many happy days together and I often wonder what became of him.

Eric Craigie, Irish Sporting Sketches

The mention of S. reminds me of one of those odd events which enable fishermen to gratify their taste for narrative without transgressing the bounds of truth. One evening, S. being with me in the boat, Patsey was regaling us from his inexhaustible store of stories as he pulled leisurely toward the house. Sport had been dull and I fancy our tactful boatman was endeavouring to lead our thoughts from disappointments to higher things. His conversation was directed over his left shoulder to S., who was in the bow, and I was often called to witness to the accuracy of his reminiscences. After many remarkable yarns Patsey began to speak of my exploits. 'Did you ever see, sir, a double-tailed fish?' 'No, Patsey.' 'Well, 'tis himself netted one there in the very bay that's before you.' 'Did you ever hear, sir, of taking three sorts of fish in the one cast?' S. had not heard of it. ''Tis himself did that same. Now, sir, did ever you know of a trout jumping into the boat to you?' S. again pleaded ignorance, and began to express a certain scepticism. Patsey, always hurt by doubt, again declared that it had happened to 'himself' (that is, to me), and said no more, though everything had happened exactly as he had stated.

The next day we fished Bally Moher. The trout were in excellent humour and Patsey was kept busy with the net — first one and then the other calling for his services — sometimes both together. I was busy with two fish, when S. called for assistance. 'Lift your hand, sir, and hold him; I'll be with you in a minute.' S. did as he was told, and a bit more; the trout made a jump, and not only came into the boat but into S.'s lap. He unhooked the fish and cast again while Patsey and I were still struggling with my brace. Immediately he had a rise at which he struck, but the playing of that fish was uncommonly heavy. It was a long time before anything was seen. Then he cried out, 'Why, I've got three!' He had, and the three were a big perch, a trout, and a lump of a roach.

After that he was gracious enough to promise that never again would he question a statement of Patsey's.

F D Barker, *An Angler's Paradise*

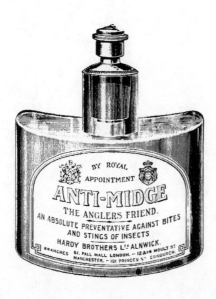

A CLARET IN CARNA

I was at Carna for a weekend once in bright sunshine and the little streams from the loughs had run to nothing. Fishing was hopeless, but I went out as usual, and, as I was walking along one of them, gossiping with the gillie, I suddenly saw a fine fresh-run sea-trout flapping on some rocks in the middle of the stream. I told the gillie to put his net over it, and when he had tapped it on the head — it weighed just three pounds — I said to him: "What fly did I catch that fish on?" He gazed at me solemnly for a second. "It was a Claret," he said. "Tomorrow there will be dozens fishing with a Claret."

Maurice Headlam, *A Holiday Fisherman*

'Did I ever tell ye the story of the trick me father once played on Major Geoghan? 'Twas many years ago now, and I was only a lad at the time.

'The Major had the little white house near the river. A great sportsman he was too, and a keen one to hunt, for all his bad sight, but 'twas the fishing he loved best.

'A queer affliction of the eyes he had, for one day he could see a fair half mile in the open and the next not more than half a yard, or a few yards at the best.

'Well, he and my father were out salmon fishing. It was one of the Major's bad days too, and well my father knew it.

'There was the Major casting away for all he was worth, and little enough did he know where his fly landed, or what became of it after.

'Now just below where he was fishing was a big lump of rocks, sticking out into the river, and 'twas in the curl behind it that the salmon lay.

'It was early spring and the river very high and strong, so me father went down below the rocks, to see if the curl was fit at all for fishing.

'Just then, what should come swirling round the corner but an old swollen corpse of a big terrier dog. Ye see it was near the time of the licence and I suppose the owner would not be inclined to pay it. One yellow ear he had, and a yellow spot on his side, and his teeth grinning the way a drowned dog's do.

'Then it was he saw the Major's fly curling about in the eddy. Now my father was fond of a joke and that gave him an idea. He gaffed the old corpse and though it wasn't nice to handle he soon had the fly fixed in its scruff, the way it would swim nicely, and pushed it out into the stream. As soon as he felt the pull, "I'm in him!" shouts the major from above, which was just what my father was waiting for.

'"Hould him, sorr — hould him!" he shouted back, "or he'll

be away in the next pool and have you destroyed."

'"I can't make him out at all," shouts the Major again. "He's as heavy as lead and not a stir out of him."

'"Bring him up to you," my father answers him, "or ye'll lose him. I know the tackle is strong."

'So the Major reels in with all his strength, and it was no light matter with the stream running, and the old dog rolling round and round and all.

'"It's the queerest fish I ever struck!" cries the Major.

'"That may well be," me father says to himself; then loud enough to be heard above the water, "Can you see him yet?"

'"See, is it?" bellows the Major. "Come on you and see for yourself. He has a tail as yellow as mustard" (that was his ear) "and rows of teeth like a shark."

'By that he had brought the dog to the bank, and was peering at it in the short-sighted way he had, poor man. "Curse ye, ye damned auld divil," he yelled, turning to me father, who had come up behind him, "I've a mind to give ye the sack."

'And with that he grinned, and the two of them set roaring with laughter.'

G D Luard, *Fishing Fortunes and Misfortunes*

"You get grand trout on the wet fly from the end of March all round here," said John Lydon, apropos of nothing except the sight of water, which always seems to make him think about fish and fishing. "Round this island and over beyond near Oughterard the catches are heavy, though I think my own favourite spot would be in Salthouse Bay or maybe Ballynalty Bay."

"And what about Golden Bay," said I. "Is that only golden to look at and not fish?"

"Indeed no," said Tom, "Golden Bay isn't a bad place for the trout at all, nor Carrig Bay either, nor Annaghkeen itself behind there."

As we made our way back to the east side of Inchagoill, where our boat was tied up at the pier, the angler's talk ranged here and there and many a story Tom had to tell.

"The best fun of all," said he, "was the jokes they used to play on poor old Mr. Brackenbury. He was often a guest of Mr. Guinness at Ashford, and a great fisherman altogether, with nothing in his head most of the time but ways and means of catching bigger fish than anybody else had ever caught. I could laugh yet when I think of the jokes Lord Oranmore and Browne, Mr. Guinness's son-in-law, used to play on the old man, and the way every time Mr. Brackenbury made a record his young Lordship would find some way of breaking it on him. When you go back to Ashford to lunch let you look into the Fish Room at the stuffed trout there in the glass case. You'll see a label on the one I mean and it will tell you that the fish weighed fifteen-and-a-half pounds and was caught by Lord Oranmore and Browne in April of 1932. There's a bit of a joke in that, I tell you."

"I think I've seen that fish already," I said, "but I don't see where the joke comes in."

"Then you couldn't have been examining it very closely," said Tom, "and that's a fact. For the fish isn't a trout at all but a spent salmon his Lordship sent up to Dublin to be stuffed, aye and painted too, the way you'd think it was a trout. And what do you think of that for a joke? Poor old Mr. Brackenbury, I can see him yet. He'd just broken the record and Ashford full of his pride and big words about it, when what does he see in front of him but this bigger fish killed only a few days afterwards. And I don't think he ever knew anything about the joke at all. I'm thinking 'twas a kind of a broken heart he had as well as a broken record."

Richard Hayward, *The Corrib Country*

'Tell Mr. Trotter about Jack and the big minnow, Patsey.' I heard Pat chuckle. 'Sure you didn't know Jackie, sir,' he said to Bob. 'He was a terrible man for turning everything into a joke, and he wasn't particular about his jokes either. Well, sir, he had a great minnow, 'twas a desperate bait. 'Twould frighten a fish entirely, the length of it. 'Twas a cold day in the month of February and he had been pike-fishing in the river below Lough Daun. 'Twas too cold for him and he came home and laid the rod on a couple of nails on the wall with the minnow hanging — he was that way, sir, with everything. Some of the lads came in and were sitting down — Jackie was after entertaining them — when one feller, Pat Keiff it was, roaring with laughter, leaned back in his chair and drove a hook of the tail triangle through the ear of him. The devil such a roar as he let out. What does Jack do but take the rod and play him above to the Doctor, the two of them roaring through the street. Sure a very careless man was Jackie.'

F D Barker, *An Angler's Paradise*

FOUR IN A ROW

My water on the Slaney ran through a valley reputed to be peopled by fairies and my best pool was named the Fairy Seat. A high diagonal weir keyed on a boulder (which was probably the Seat) sent the stream slanting across to hit against the far bank and run parallel with it over a nest of rocks which gave ideal lies. Standing on one identical spot I once hooked and landed in rapid succession four spring fish with not more than three or four casts intervening between landing one and hooking the next. My upstream neighbour, who was not devoid of jealousy, was watching through field glasses and her remarks were retailed gleefully to me next day by her companion. "Good, Kingie is in a fish". "My God, the judge has got another". "The bloody fellow has hooked a third". "This is too much, the bastard has a fourth".

T H Kingsmill Moore, *A Man May Fish*

One day when the river was high and coloured Tom and I were sitting by The Pool on a grassy bank watching Dick at work. He was casting an exceptionally heavy minnow, and the sight of it must have touched some chord in Tom's memory. He looked up at me sideways, from beneath the peak of his old tweed cap, and I knew a story was coming.

'That's a great lump of a bait the master's fishing with. Och, I'm not saying at all it's too big for the way the river is this day,' he added, ''tis only it chanst to put me in mind of Denny Power.

'You'll have seen Denny Power, him that keeps the public-house at the corner of the village. He's an old man now, but you can tell from the big frame of him what he must have been. Red hair, he used to have, and big hairy wrists. He was terrible strong and the wildest lad I ever saw when he had a drop of drink taken.

'He was a grand fisherman too, and could sling a heavy salmon-bait across the Big River, fair-and-square on to the far bank, any wide place you'd care to name.

'I'll say, too, he wasn't always caring greatly whose water the salmon he caught came from, and he caught a fair share of them.

'Now there's a deep hole above the bridge, below the village. Yourself must know it well, of course. I wouldn't say it was free water, but 'tis rarely fished by them that has the rights, for except when the water's very high, and clear as well, 'tis useless to fish it. The fish are there all the same, and big ones at that. Often's the times I've seen them rolling there like a lot of hogs.

'This was Denny's favourite spot, and right or wrong, when the water was in order, many's the salmon he had out of it.

'One year an Englishman had the fishing of it, a small dark mean-eyed little man that expected thirty shillings' worth for every pound he spent, as well I know, having been employed by him for a season, and jealous as hell of anyone else's luck. Now walking down the bank one day, Denny had seen a monster of a fish disporting himself in the pool, and had made up his mind, by hook or crook, to have him out of it. One afternoon a day or two later, he had just returned from a fair and had some drink taken, the amount of drink that only sharpened his wits and didn't affect his legs at all, when a gossoon comes running up the hill to him on his doorstep shouting, "The Englishman have a great fish hooked in the big hole above; he's as big as an ass — he threw a lep and I saw him."

'"Hell," roars Denny. "The bloody thief — 'tis my fish, he have!" and with that he dives into his house, and in two-three minutes out he comes with his bait rod and gaff. 'Twas the stoutest rod I ever saw (he kept it always mounted to save time), and dangling from the end of it a spoon bait as big as your hand fixed straight on to the line without any trace, and a mass of lead strung above it.

'"We'll bloody soon see whose fish it is," he stormed, and pushing through the crowd of us at the bar entry he hurried down to the bridge.

'We could not think what he had in mind at all, but well we knew that Denny was sure to provide sport.

'In two minutes we were on the bridge and there sure enough was the Englishman, his rod bent double and the big fish ploughing about somewhere in the depths of the hole.

'And there on the opposite bank was Denny Power, slinging out his great spoon for all he was worth, and it making slaps like a plate when it hit the water — and he all the while cursing and swearing at the Englishman on the other side.

'At last he made an extra long cast right in behind where the Englishman's line cut the water. Of course the two lines soon crossed, and the hooks of the spoon caught firm in the dropper which the little Englishman had on.

'"I'm in him," yells Denny in triumph, and started to reel in as hard as he could. Nothing could stand against that rod and line.

'There was the three of them all pulling different ways. The little man didn't know what to do. First he held hard till we thought his rod would break. Then whether he gave up, for a minute, or his hand slipped, I couldn't say.

'Anyway there was an awful screech from his reel, and as Denny reeled in harder than ever, the Englishman's line came streeling out, and gradually, for all its struggling and splashings, the fish was drawn in, gaffed, and thrown on the grass.

'"Whose fish is it now?" Denny bellowed. Then he carefully cut off the little man's cast with his knife and let the line go.

'The Englishman, dancing with rage, and swearing he'd have the law of Denny — but all Denny did was smile and take off his hat.

'We carried the salmon up to the village, and weighed it at the butcher's. Thirty-six pounds he weighed and he as bright as a new shilling.

'Then what must Denny do, but pack up the great fish in a bass and send it back to the Englishman, cast and all attached, with a polite note by the hands of that same gossoon that brought him the news.'

G D Luard, *Fishing Fortunes and Misfortunes*

I remember another day of foul weather when Patsey and I were driven off Inchicrag to take refuge on the river. To be honest, nothing of interest happened on this day; I only mention it because it reminds me of Jackie and some of his stories. We had not fished the first pool when we were compelled to take shelter under an overhanging crag from the driving rain. Patsey had no more than got his pipe into action when we heard the crashing of brambles, and a prolonged r__r__ip followed by an inelegant remark, addressed to no one in particular. The next moment Jackie, Patsey's eldest brother, stumbled into our retreat. Half the skirt of his rain-coat was flapping round his feet, but he was, as usual, cheerful. Nothing was ever able to damp Jackie's spirits.

At this time he was fully engaged in mothering two inexperienced sportsmen from Lancashire and, for want of something better to do had taken them into the bogs to shoot. While I was pinning up his coat — which he was all for cutting off — I asked if he had been having any sport. 'Sport, is it!' he returned, in his rapid jerky manner of speech; 'devil a better, sir. Sure the young one was twice in bog-holes yesterday, below at Bally Portree. 'Twas twenty minutes we were scraping him. Sure one suit of his clothes is that shrunk 'twouldn't hold Mickey Ryan, that's but a slip of a lad.' 'Yes, but did you get any birds?' 'Don't mention it, sir! Birds? devil a feather but one did we knock at all — an old coot that Father Haley was after crippling last Sunday.' 'I heard you shooting.' 'Why wouldn't you? Never fear but there was shooting and plenty. The devil as much powder was burnt since the last Boer War!' 'Where are they now, Jack?' 'Begor, I dunno. They were worm-fishing below in the big hole. Have ye a fill of the pipe, Patsey?'

One of the Lancastrians could cast a fly and, given a chance, would have taken a share of the trout, but he of the shrunken suit could *not* put his cast within yards of the wished-for spot. What time Jack was not picking the flies out of the fisher's coat he was disengaging them from his own clothing and flesh. One evening, just as it was getting dark, Patsey and I were at the river's mouth when we were joined by Jack and his party. The man who could fish was in the bow of the boat, the other was under Jackie's immediate eye. The evening's amusement must have been planned in advance. For a fourth fly had been added to the pupil's cast, and Patsey (evidently in the know) observed quietly to me, 'We'll be after having a diversion, sir.'

At the point opposite the heap of stones was a large waterlogged thorn-bush — left there by the last flood — scarcely to be seen in the dim light. Getting the boat where he wanted it, Jack, in a low excited voice, called to his pupil, 'Cast there, sir, there, into that dark spot, there's a whacker! Again, sir, again! cast over him, sir!' A pause — then 'Raise your hand, sir; raise your hand, sir!' At the same time he gave the boat a sly pull with the oars and away went the reel as merrily as you could wish. 'He has him in the bush,' Patsey whispered. It was exceedingly well done; the bush gave and sprang, the reel ran and the fisher wound; Jackie gave directions and enlarged encouragingly upon the size of the fish. Meanwhile we escaped to a distance where our laughter could not be heard.

F D Barker, *An Angler's Paradise*

"*Irish Boatman* (surveying the solitary result of the day): It's a foine fish for the size of ut: them'll run about three to a pound.
  Angler: Hardly that, I should say.
  Boatman: Well, maybe the other two'd be a bit bigger."

Punch

Jonah Barrington was no angler, but a cosmopolitan lawyer and observer of eighteenth century Irish life whose Personal Sketches of his Own Times *is required reading for anyone with an interest in things Irish. This extract shows why.*

In the year 1800, a labourer dwelling near the town of Athy, County Kildare, (where some of my family then resided) was walking with his comrade up the banks of the Barrow to the farm of a Mr. Richardson, on whose meadows they were employed to mow; each, in the usual Irish way, having his scythe loosely wagging over his shoulder, and lazily lounging close to the bank of the river, they espied a salmon partly hid under the bank. It is the nature of this fish that, when his *head* is concealed, he fancies no one can see his *tail* (there are many wise-acres, besides the salmon, of the same way of thinking). On the present occasion the body of the fish was visible.

'Oh Ned — Ned dear!' said one of the mowers, 'Look at that big fellow there — isn't it a pity we ha'nt no spear?'

'May be,' said Ned, 'we could be after picking the lad with the scythe-handle.'

'True for you!' said Dennis: 'the spike of yeer handle is longer nor mine; give the fellow a dig with it at any rate.'

'Ay, will I,' returned the other: 'I'll give the lad a prod he'll never forget any how.'

The spike and their sport was all they thought of: but the *blade* of the scythe, which hung over Ned's shoulders, never came into the contemplation of either of them. Ned cautiously looked over the bank; the unconscious salmon lay snug, little imagining the conspiracy that had been formed against his tail.

'Now hit the lad smart!' said Dennis: 'there now — there! rise your fist: now you have the boy! now Ned — success!'

Ned struck at the salmon with all his might and main, and that was not trifling. But whether 'the boy' was picked or not never appeared: for poor Ned, bending his neck as he struck at the salmon, placed the vertebrae in the most convenient position for unfurnishing his shoulders: and his head came tumbling splash into the barrow, to the utter astonishment of his comrade, who could not conceive *how* it could *drop off* so suddenly. But the next minute he had the consolation of seeing the head attended by *one of his own ears,* which had been most dexterously sliced off by the same blow which beheaded his comrade.

The head and ear rolled down the river in company, and were picked up with extreme horror at the mill-dam, near Mr. Richardson's, by one of the miller's men.

'Who the devil does this head belong to' exclaimed the miller.

'Whoever owned it,' said the man, 'had three ears, at any rate.'

Sir Jonah Barrington, *Personal Sketches of His Own Times*

It will take years to efface the clinging memories of my first adventure with a dry fly. When I went forth equipped with all the latest scientific implements to perform, preening myself that I, and I alone, amongst my many angling acquaintances, was IT — the immaculate Purist. The angels must have been watching and smiling. Heaven must have rung with their mirth before the day was ended, for, I suppose, like mortals here below, they derive a lot of amusement out of a poor devil's discomfiture.

It was on a Monday morning. I got up early intending to go to work. I had to search for a pen-knife that I had mislaid, and found it in the drawer in which I kept my tackle. In a weak moment I picked up an aluminium box containing dry flies, with glass lids covering the various compartments; I sat down, wrapt in admiration, as I gazed on the lovely little creations. Then by some process of reasoning I concluded that I would be many a day in the grave pushing up the daisies, when one day stolen for sport wouldn't make much difference one way or the other. If my enthusiasm hadn't been overproof I would have taken warning at the omens of misfortune that crossed my path before I got clear of the street I live in. When I opened the door the first person I saw was a woman pushing a handcart full of apples; her hair was as russet as the bloom on some of the fruit in the cart. In the casual glance I got of her I noticed a shade over one of her eyes. I would never have thought again of the incident had she not in passing wished me luck.

Half way down the street I noticed a gentleman knocking at a door on the opposite side. It was with a twinge of regret that I noticed he was a clergyman. Though I give first to no one in my respect for the cloth, I would sooner have met him when I was returning than when just setting out for the day on my maiden trip as an exponent of a new cult.

Far be it from me to suggest that meeting the reverend gentleman would bring me bad luck, but my father often said that the day you are sure to have Will-o'-the-Wisp's blessing (that is, an empty bag and a wet foot), it is part of the ritual that you meet his reverence before the pipe you lit at your own door is empty.

The journey seemed very long; the old steam engine hissed and coughed up the tiresome climb from Tallaght to Brittas. The sharp walk of a mile from Blessington brought on a happy frame of mind. Just as I sighted the scene of my objective, I was thrown into a fit of depression by the sight of a chattering pin-feathered magpie.

It was then it dawned on me that the appointed day in my career had arrived, when I was to be the laughing stock of the devil and all his imps.

Short was my shadow on Burgidge Bridge where the Liffey and King's River meet when I put the rod together. An up stream breeze was faintly rippling a good depth of water in the pool below. Fish were rising freely near both banks. The fly on the water I never thought of, but choosing my quarry, a quick riser at the near bank, I put a match to the briar as I waded in to fight the fates arrayed against me, shouting "muck for luck", as I mounted a cow dung fly. After a few unsuccessful attempts I got it up to him at last. In his innocence he sucked it down. Did I strike? No. My surprise was so great that my arm remained like unto the right one on Grattan's Statue outside Trinity College, Dublin. Back came my fly to the surface, and with it a tiny bubble to mock me for the idiot that I was.

I fished another rise, determined to correct the non-striking habit if I got a chance, which I truly did. I got a side view of him as he took the fly. With the left hand I pulled in the slack and with the other I struck with all the speed I was master of. He was for making a fight, but I wasn't in the humour of indulging in any of the finer tactics of the game — giving him line or playing. I yanked him out with a jerk, swinging him high in the air against the parapet of the bridge twenty feet above me. The resounding thud re-echoed from the wall. Then I marvelled at the nerve I showed in defying convention. My ecstasy had a short life.

Walking along the bank a few minutes after this success, carrying the rod in the left hand, I fell into a deep, disused rabbit burrow. The top of the rod caught in a wire fence that ran between me and the water. I broke it clean across above the second ferrule. I wedged it in and lashed it on as best I could, determined to carry on, though well I knew the witch's brew was simmering. Inside the next hour I tore the back out of a new mackintosh on a barbed wire fence, and punctured my right rubber thigh boot on a sharp branch in the bank. I did not know until I waded in to cast a fly over to the far side, when I felt the shock of the cold water pouring in on my warm foot. I am not going to record the many times my fly was hung up in obstructions that at other times in wet fly fishing I would have missed, or will I tell of the many breakages of casts or loss of flies. Needless to relate my stock of both was sadly depleted after all I went through. I have faithfully noted my misfortunes in the order they occurred, so I suppose that it was fitting that the climax of my blunders — if blunders you can call them — should be reached just after I gave up in dismay, and plodded my way across the fields to catch the steam tram for home and comfort.

To apprise the extent of my final catastrophe it is necessary that I describe an instrument that I had some time previously constructed. The reason it was ever fashioned was to do away with a cumbersome landing net which caused me endless worry by catching in briars, shrubs and fences.

Once when looking at a very large triple pike hook I conceived the idea of inserting the shank of it into a piece of light cane a yard and a half long. I lashed it with wax end to secure it firmly. Next I bored a hole in a cork bung, and passed it through from the other end of the cane, embedding it firmly in the barbs of the hooks as a protection.

This substitute for a net I called a lifter or trout gaff. When I first removed the rod from its cover I placed the cane handle into one of the compartments and secured it to the left lapel of my mack, and also below the bottom button with two safety pins. I was quite proud of the idea. Little did I think that I had forged another link in the chain of mistakes that eventually went so near to encompass my destruction. When crossing an earthen ditch on top of which was placed a lot of freshly cut whitehorn bushes, all the butts pointing in the same direction and firmly sodded in; I slipped and fell across it. The cover caught in the bushes, and when I strove to rise the barb of the hook came through my cheek and got securely fastened in my upper lip.

The bung got knocked off the barbs when I fell. I gave another frantic plunge to try and rise, which only drove the hook further in till it grated on my poor teeth. Imagine my horror when I found that I couldn't get up or slip back. I prayed with a devotion that was both earnest and fervent for deliverance from my crucifixion.

As I lay there the thought crossed my mind: "was this to be my miserable ending," to be found dead on top of a ditch in the wilds of Baltyboys?

Then I remembered having a knife, and luckily I found it in my right hand coat pocket. I opened it as I lay there and severed the cover and cane. I struggled to my feet a free man once more with a foot of cane hanging to my upper lip. I went down on my knees and offered a prayer of thanksgiving for the freedom I had regained.

I made my way to the nearest farmhouse. When I appeared in the doorway the sole occupant, an elderly man, roared out some words in Irish and bolted into the bedroom with fright when he saw the streams of blood and the pendulum swinging from my upper lip. I borrowed his mirror off the wall, and brought it out into the sunlight. Then I cut the lashing at the end of the cane and inserted the blade of the knife and released it, leaving the pike hook for the doctor in Blessington to remove.

A car passed along the road, and the occupants observing my predicament, gave me a lift to the doctor to be operated on. The local M.D. was away on holidays when I arrived there. A lady doctor was deputising for him, and to her lot fell the task of freeing me.

She tried to cut the hook with a pliers and pull the broken part through, but couldn't manage it. She had to dig through the sinews of the lip eventually, and the lance she used was as blunt as a table knife. After untold agonies the hole was large enough for me to push the hook upward and release it. She persuaded me to take a restorative like a seidlitz powder from a long glass phial. I must have drank it too quickly, for the breath left me and I remembered no more.

After coming to I suffered from a headache and had to rush away to catch the steam tram poorer by half a guinea.

The foregoing incidents happened a few years ago, and lately I flattered myself that I had lived down the idle rumours that were floating about after the occurrence.

But I got a rude shock when passing through Blessington recently, when I heard someone shouting "There's the fellow who gaffed himself."

Laurie Gaffey, *A Freelance Angler in Ireland*

Fishing was reserved for the holidays when, a suitable rod having at last been acquired, I roamed the countryside on a bicycle, stopping at any bridge over a likely stream and casting my fly where I fancied. Only once was I questioned. I had unlimbered to fish a deep pool in Donegal where first a white trout of a pound, and then one of over two pounds, came to me. As I was landing the second fish a bailiff approached and asked me for my licence. Of course I had not got one, and I said quite truthfully that I had come to fish for brown trout. He smiled. He had heard that one before. But all he said was "There's another good pool round the corner" and left. Forty years later he gave evidence before me in a fishery case. I had no recollection of him and asked if there was a good run of white trout in a certain river. "Faith and there is, and your lordship wouldn't be long in whipping them out" was his disconcerting answer. He had recognised the poacher turned gamekeeper. He did not omit to tell counsel, nor have counsel allowed me to forget.

T H Kingsmill Moore, *A Man May Fish*

WIND AND WEATHER

CHAPTER 4

As an element, water has its own perils. Combined with wind and rain, to which the Irish angler is no stranger, many of Ireland's great lochs and rivers can, and do, become the Jekyll to Hyde's placid exterior. The yearly toll of those who drown in the ostensibly harmless act of angling, bears mute and tragic witness to the dangers of water.

No-one has explained these or illustrated them better than A A Luce. 'Caught in a storm' is a vivid reminder of how treacherous lochs such as Conn may become within minutes. Few anglers who venture on the great western lochs have not had somewhat similar experiences. And let the wise shake their heads at F D Barker's foolhardiness on 'Inchicrag'.

During a certain September there were two whole days of heavy rain with a gale from the south-west. As a consequence the river was over its banks in many places. Though the rain had ceased twenty-four hours before, the gale was still with us. Patsey remembers that day vividly — he tells of it to each newcomer — it was the day when I won his confidence in boatmanship.

In the hall of the Grey House we held consultation, and decided on the river. 'Sure the lake is covered with waterspouts' was Pat's report; we could see them from the study window chasing each other past the end of Wood Island. As we came out of the door Patsey started off up the avenue. 'Where are you going, Patsey?' 'To the river, sir; where else would I go?' 'Yes, but I'm not walking.' 'How will you be going, sir?' 'In the boat.'

'The boat, sir! Sure the boat wouldn't stop on the lake; it wouldn't float ten minutes.' However, I insisted, and very unwillingly he went with me to the bank above the boat-house. It was certainly rough. The little whirlwinds were spinning and dancing until they broke on the far shore. The air was thick with a mist, the waves were up amongst the trees of the island, and the spray was everywhere drifting in light clouds. But I had no fancy for the long walk. With a little care I thought that I could make a fair wind of it if I could but get a little to the east for a start. 'Patsey man, can you take the boat as far as the point of the island?' 'I can, sir; but what will you do then? Sure it's not the island at all you'll be wanting.' 'No, Patsey, it's the river, and we'll not be long getting there either.' For the first bit we had the shelter of the land, but even there a sea was running and the wind came in heavy blasts. Patsey kept on gamely, glancing at me over his shoulder from time to time, his white head bare, 'the hat' on the floor of the boat, safely under one foot. When there was room enough I told him to raise the oars clear of the water, and upon no account to let them down. All we had to do then was to go before the wind fast enough to get away from the following seas. So I stood up at my steering oar and squared away for the river, opening my oilskin coat whenever there was need for a little more speed. Certain it is that Pat's boat had never travelled so fast before. I kept so close to the point, west of the castle, as to scrape the end of the starboard oar — which was a further shock to my crew — but I wanted all the room there was. I don't think Pat knew when we entered the river, for his eyes were fixed on me all the time. 'Faith, the first thing I knew was a bump, and we were above in the big hole, the bow of her in the bank, as nice as you please, beside a little quay of turf, and what to do but step out of her? 'Twas forty miles an hour we went — faith, a steamboat wouldn't go faster.' Before he got up, however, he said to me: 'After that, sir, I'll go with you where you like, devil a fear but I will. I went because you would go, but I never thought 'twas to the river we'd get at all, but to the bottom entirely. I'm your man, sir.'

F D Barker, *An Angler's Paradise*

'The yellow gleam of wrecking rock' — with one telling phrase, A A Luce conjures vividly all the considerable dangers of the great western lochs — in this case, Loch Mask.

And now a word about engine-craft and boat-craft; for there is more to learn about the western lakes than the art of catching fish in them. When running the engine between the drifts in a moderate wave, drive straight into the wave, as far as possible; it is safest and driest, and keeps the boat steady in its whole length, and there is little or no splash. If the wave is heavy, slow down. Driven fast against a high wave, the boat rears up like a mettled horse, and the bow comes crashing down, shivering the timbers and opening the seams, and the bow thwart will break if a heavy weight is on it. Run slow, but not too slow, lest the engine stall. A following wind is heady, like champagne, and, like it, calls for care. The boat is soon running at twenty miles per hour, and when the wave gets long and steep, the boat may side-slip on the crest and slither down the slope. Slow down at once. Side winds are a special study. Usually one can drive with safety down the long furrow with a wall of water on either side; but watch the crest of the wave, and if it looks like breaking, take no chance; go slow. A side wave can sometimes be negotiated in corkscrew fashion, like a crab. There is a big wave a-beam that looks threatening; sidestep into it; the boat will rise to it; then straighten out again into the long furrow, till the next big one comes along; then repeat the manoeuvre. The ancient Greeks thought that every third wave was the big one, and they gave it a name; on the western lakes the rhythm of the big wave is nearer one in seven than one in three.

Head wind, side wind and following wind — each one has its thrills and its dangers. Experience soon teaches how to deal with them. Boats are built to float, and provided your boat is seaworthy, broad in the beam, with a good deep keel, and provided the helmsman keeps cool and the children do not stand up or panic, all will be well. The worst situation to meet is the huddle of waters; you meet it rounding a point on a gusty day; wind and wave come at you on both sides all at once; and you have hardly time to think or take your bearings; in such a case shut off the engine at once, and leave it to the gillie. Boats are made to float, and they do float; they right themselves in a wonderful way, provided they are given time, and are not forced at speed.

And now for boat-craft. Boat-craft proper is much more than pulling an oar or a pair of oars; it is managing the boat like an artist or craftsman; it involves a certain oneness between boat and boatman; for he must express himself, his intentions and purpose, in the movements of his boat. King Solomon found three things too wonderful for him, yea four which he knew not — and one of the four was the way of a ship in the midst of the sea. Watch the bow of the violin in the hand of the *maestro,* or the fingers of the organist on the keys of the cathedral organ, and watch the oars in Michael's hands. King Solomon had seen his proud ship of Tarshish in full sail with its cargo of ivory, of apes and peacocks; and a gallant sight it was. Michael's way with his boat on a drift on Lough Conn is a thing of wonder, too.

Gillies do not pull a very strong oar, as a rule; they eat so little meat, and their technique in pulling is not what it might be. The College student in his old school tie or boatclub tie, down for the fishing, will beat the gillie in the boat race at the local regatta; but the gillie has what the student cannot have, boat-craft. The gillie is one with his boat; he is born to it; in action his two oars are extensions of his two arms; to see what should be done, and to do it, with him are one and the same thing. In the tricky launching or landing, when strong winds are blowing athwart, he seems to feel the boat as a whole; he knows the exact position and angle of bow and stern and centre; he reckons sub-consciously with currents and sideblast; he feels in his bones the amount of freeboard, and the strike of the wind on bow and stern; he is one with his boat; if he shifts his seat, or bids you do so, that is the reason why.

On the drift his craft rises to the level of an art, and anglers often owe fish to the gillie's art as well as to their own. Seated towards the stern on the last thwart but one, the gillie angles the boat to the breeze, bow-in for an in-shore breeze, bow-out for an off-shore breeze. With one oar or scull out behind he is in full control; with one push in she goes; with one pull out she comes, no matter how high the wave. If you want fish on the western lakes, you must cast near the rocks, and the gillie has one eye on the look-out for the yellow gleam of wrecking rock. In a very light breeze he works sideways, like a crab; he makes the most of every flurry of air; and often it is his oar that imparts to your fly the twist or turn that gives you a trout.

A A Luce, *Fishing and Thinking*

Let me round off the picture of my friend with a true story of a storm on the lake. This is an aspect of a gillie's life that fair-weather anglers and river anglers do not see. We learn to appreciate our gillies, when we realise that their job has its dangers that form character, and display it.

Few gillies can swim, and on the whole it is better so; the non-swimmer will not let himself be caught, if he can help it, in a situation that calls for swimming; he will not expose himself or you to danger; he trusts his boat, and he means to stay in it till he reaches land. Water is his friend and ally, not an enemy; when he is water-borne, he is in his element; he has been at the job since boyhood; it is second nature to him to do the right thing in a crisis; he understands wind and wave, and the way of a small boat in a big storm; he would not be there with you if there were any real danger. Given a good boat, two pairs of strong oars, resolute arms, stout hearts and cool heads, anglers on the western lakes will make shelter, even if they cannot reach all at once 'The haven where they would be'.

Courage and coolness are great qualities in a gillie, and you do not really know your man till you have been with him in a storm. Nothing tests a man like danger to life. I knew a boatman on Lough Mask who went as white as a sheet when a stiff nor-wester blew down Mountrasna Bay, and the waves were topped with white. It was no place for him, and he was not typical. Most gillies have cool heads and hearts of oak. They must have these qualities; to be cool and courageous is part of their job. Anglers want fish, and are often willing to take a chance. Whatever precautions are taken, you may be caught at a disadvantage. Storms arise suddenly; winds swing round, and plans 'go all a'gley'. When that happens, the courage required is not the active heroism of the soldier in action; but it is resolution, the ability to be calm and cool and collected. On a stormy lake there is little one can *do*; man cannot pit his puny strength against wind and wave; he cannot *fight* the forces of nature; he must *use* them; and that means keeping calm and cool, and doing the right thing at the right time.

Michael and I have shared not a few anxious moments — moments that to me were anxious; but I never once saw him flustered, much less frightened; in a tight corner he always seems to have something in reserve. His worst day on the lake is worth describing. He has often told me about it in general terms, such as, 'The lake went up in smoke that day, Sir.' The angler who was with him in the adventure wrote an account of it at the time, and he has shown me the record, and it is frightening still.

It was the day of an angling competition in April, 1943. The rendezvous was Coryosla Bay at the Pontoon end of Lough Conn, some eight miles by water from Cloghans, where Michael lives. It was wartime, and there was no petrol for outboard engines or for driving round by road. After breakfast Frank, a young engineer, and Michael set off in their good, solid nineteen-foot boat; it was a calm morning, and Brendan, Michael's son, decided to go, too, in Michael's dinghy on the chance of a job as gillie. The dinghy was little more than a canoe, about twelve feet long, as light as a cork, with an up-turned prow at either end, like a Viking ship; it was meant for coasting about in sheltered bays in fair weather. They reached Coryosla without incident in a couple of hours; but clouds were piling up in the south; the wind was freshening; and the men knew that they were in for it. The competition gun was fired, and the anglers started work; but almost immediately the storm broke, and very soon fishing was out of the question. Lashed by wind and rain the boats ran for the nearest shelter, and tied up; anglers and gillies took refuge in hospitable cottages, where they found a welcome, warmth and tea. All the afternoon the storm raged, but lulled off about 6 p.m. Then Frank, Michael and Brendan forgathered at Coryosla and held a council of war. The issue was simple — eight easy-looking miles by water, or a trudge of twice that distance on a rough and stony road, with the prospect of returning on the morrow for boats and gear. The wind was still strong, but southerly; it should be with them all the way; rowing would be easy, and if all went well, they would be safe and sound at home within an hour and a half. That is better than a four hours' trudge, is it not? The *ayes* have it. They decided that all three should go in the big boat, and take the dinghy in tow.

For a while they were in sheltered water, and all went well; but as they drew out into the open lake, the wave was longer, and the dinghy began to misbehave. Towing is never easy in a wave; in a high and following wave it is almost impossible. Now the light dinghy would overrun and bump; now it would act as a sail and confuse the steering. To weight it and control it Michael volunteered to enter the towed dinghy and guide it with an oar. He did so, and found that he could guide it up to a point, but not control it; for as the wave grew steeper, the dinghy would poise like a surf-board on the white crest of a breaking wave, and then come sliding down the forward slope and crash against the boat. It was a terrible position for them all. Frank and Brendan shouted to Michael to come back into the comparative safety of the boat and cut the dinghy adrift. He would not hear of it; he stayed in the dinghy, cut the tow rope, and pulled clear. It was a high act of cool and calculated courage. The two men were in a solid boat with a good keel and considerable freeboard, and if they shipped a sea, the one could bale, while the other rowed; but Michael was alone in a cockle-shell, alone in the middle of an angry lake; his craft had little or no freeboard; it could spin round at a touch, and if it met a breaker broadside on, it would swamp instantaneously. But Michael never relaxed for a moment; he kept his head, and, watching every wave like a lynx, by sheer boatcraft he remained in full control of his frail barque.

An hour passed, and now in the gathering gloom the following wind had brought boat and dinghy to a point within half a mile of Rinmore Point, and if they could round that headland, there lay safety and a lee shore. Suddenly the wind failed them, and veered; the south wind that had blown all day dropped, and there was for a few moments an oily calm, an ominous calm, more fearsome than the storm; away to the west, high up in the sky over the shoulder of Mount Nephin, appeared the lurid red glow that told of a change of wind and of a hurricane on the way. They pulled frantically; for they were abreast the long, pitiless Brackwanshagh Reef. The last few yards made all the difference. They had just cleared the reef, and had entered Storm Bay, when they heard a rumble; and with a roar like an express train a tornado from the west struck the lake. Then (in the words of Frank's record) 'The squall hit us in a cloud of spray. It enveloped us completely and sent us hurtling towards the shore. All I could do was to keep our stern square to the wind. I kicked my rubber boots off. Soon the boat was travelling at such speed that I feared she would split in two when the crash came. A thole-pin broke, and I lost the last vestige of control. Suddenly Brendan started; he saw the line of white breakers ahead. I felt the keel grating on the rocks. Then a great wave took us up and hurled us broadside-on right over the rocks and into the sandy pool beyond. Twenty yards away we could dimly see Michael calmly tying up his tiny dinghy.'

A A Luce, *Fishing and Thinking*

MAINLY DESCRIPTIVE

CHAPTER 5

'Water,' wrote Stephen Gwynn, 'affects my whole consciousness with a pleasure that is not exclusive, for other things can enhance it, but that nothing can replace.' How true that is, and how true the magical evocation of that 'influence which tranquillises rather than stimulates, and makes the mind extraordinarily receptive of beauty.'

Angling surely is as much about the lingering of time and the beauty of place as it is about fish. Indeed, the older we grow, the more the former advances and the latter recedes. How many of us identify with the words of Sir Thomas Grattan Esmonde: 'And the mountains to the west stand out black as ebony, with a fringe of fire, and the eastern hills light up in the afterglow; and then the gorgeous spectacle fades away.' Or with the lady angler on Cloon Lake in Kerry who, as her day on the lake ended, turned and cried to the water, 'You've been very good to us'.

As I got out of the boat, the sun was nearly down, a little west of the Twelve Pins. They stood out now, absolutely clear cut, a jagged solid mass, purple as a plum. To my right, the moor, a huge expanse, was ringed about by hills, olive-brown as the bog grass; the western horizon was luminous and golden. But it was one of the moments when colour shifts as you watch it; I walked towards the sun; it had sunk before I reached the lake, but there was still a golden ray on the water. Far from me, I could distinguish on that lucent sheen the broken line where the stream entered, and I pushed down the boat and pulled towards it. Everything was extraordinarily still and tranquil: even a leaping fish broke the silence, and my oars seemed to make absolute tumult. I landed, and my fishing was over in five minutes: it had given me only the pleasure which every angler knows of straightening a line over a swift run of water; but it had, as so often happens with fishing, made an errand which led me into the heart of beauty.

As I paddled back, I saw the sky changed: radiations like an aurora shot up through the ruddy gold. The little lake on which I was led by a narrow cut into a larger one, and along that whole vista of water the sky's colours were reflected, under the sombre purple of heathy banks. I stowed the boat safe and took the footpath home across that solitude — leagues of it on every side, where "Only God exults in silence over fields no man may reap."

So the poet had written for my reading of that afternoon, and though it is only now I think of his line, perhaps he had affected my mood. To the south-west was a planet, glorious and golden; to the north-east, over the hills that run down from Joyce Country towards Screeb and Costello, another star answered it. A grouse crew in the heather to my right. I had been walking southward, but as I started to pull back I faced north, and saw again the sunset glory. It spread beyond the Twelve Pins; and just where the Joyce Country mountains over Maam joined in to them was a region of half-light, delicate and wonderful; a glimmer rather than a glow. These mountains were not solid and purple, as were the Pins; they had a colour ill-defined and tremulous that was neither green nor grey nor brown, yet had something of them all; and it passed imperceptibly into the long range of unlighted slopes and skyline. I pulled fast across, rounded the points as neatly as I could, and made for the quay; but as I slackened to enter, the beauty I looked at held me. I could not go in, but paddled out again and lay on my oars. It was dark now; the island mass with its trees seemed inky blackness; yet as one looked one saw it was all green — water, ilex-trees, mountains beyond, and sky. Overhead, stars grew thick; the grouse's call came again across the water, and a mallard quacked. From the upper island a heron flapped out squawking; and behind all these was the steady roar of a distant waterfall. I stayed there in a sort of dream, half anxious to go before the spell had ceased to hold me, yet unwilling to shorten such an hour. Water has for me at least an odd magic: it affects my whole consciousness with a pleasure that is not exclusive, for other things can enhance it, but that nothing can replace. The sea is different: it heightens one's sense of vitality; it has its own joy; but its strong breath does not blend so subtly with a mood as do the exhalations of clean unspoilt lake or river — above all, when the scent of turf is in the air. Never had I felt more strongly than this day the influence which tranquillises rather than stimulates, and makes the mind extraordinarily receptive of beauty. Probably if we could read our own impulses it is this emanating charm which accounts for the wise folly of fishermen. I was glad to have caught a salmon again after a long spell of lost opportunities; the sea-trout one has taken are a gracious dish for dinner; but what turned my day into something happy and memorable was my wild-goose chase across the moor, and my solitary paddling in that dewy twilight.

Stephen Gwynn, *Duffer's Luck*

The other rivers in Ireland that we fished with the dry-fly were like nothing that I have seen in England. They had a character of their own, "eigenartich" as the Germans say, something peculiar to themselves — the Brosna, the Silver River, the upper Suck, the bog-stream at Kildangan, the Dee of the County Louth. The Brosna held fine trout and some peal (as they call grilse in Ireland). But it was thoroughly poached and it was rather too big to be an ideal dry-fly river, so, attractive though it was, we did not go there much after we discovered the Silver River.

It should rather have been called the Golden River, for its water was the real deep brown of the true bogland and showed clear gold, when the sun shone, over the white sand of the shallows. No doubt that sand, exposed and white and gleaming when the river shrank in high summer, gave it the name of Silver — every little seaside place in Ireland has its Silver Strand. But it is always associated in my mind with the dark brown of the deep stretches where the big trout lay, rather than with silver; with absolute solitude — only twice did I meet human beings on its banks in many visits; with vast miles of heather stretching level to a blue hill on the horizon; and with the most poisonous midges and horse-flies in Ireland.

Unlike many Irish bogs, it was not dotted with cottages. There was one farm-house on the banks of the stream to which certain annoying ducks belonged, but I never saw a human soul either inside or out. And there must have been cattle above, for sometimes the river came down muddy when they had been standing and champing in the water to get away from the flies and the heat. Once a local angler arrived, and was much annoyed to find us. But we had leave to fish from the owner (as was not always the case), and he could say nothing. He went away after telling us that the fish in this river always stopped rising at ten minutes past nine every night, and I always regret that we never noticed what they did when summer time came in: did they keep

"God's time or Protestant time" — which was the Irish antithesis? I shall never know.

Another time, when the water was muddied by the cattle and we had gone upstream, away from the best places — many miles, it seemed, in the heat — and were resting under one of the rare thorn bushes, but still below the polluting cattle, we were surprised by an elegant apparition in white kid gloves, attended by a man carrying his expensive rod, and landing net, and large lunch. We were so indignant at the completeness of this angler, at his cool appearance, at the unfair protection of his hands from horse-flies, that we, selfishly enough, let him go past us away from the water which we knew to be good for three-pounders. After all, there *might* be as good places above — let us hope he found it so: at any rate, we never saw him again, and we were never bothered again by fishermen, natives or visitors. Probably the little river was too far away for the natives. It was a long journey, when the motor was not so easily available, and they probably did not think it worth while to go so far, especially as the Brosna, a bigger river open to everyone, as is usual in Ireland, was at the very doors of the village.

So we used to start out alone in the morning from our unpretentious little inn, through the wide, dirty, village street, with its ass-carts and pigs and potato sacks: the straw and the dust blowing in our faces or behind us, for it is rarely windless in Ireland. Beyond the bridges over the big river and the railway, the road bends to the right round the "demesne," the trees of which, neglected and covered with moss and lichen, lean through the broken fence over the road. Then the corner is turned, and, after the canal, there is nothing but flat bog as far as the eye can see. Mile after mile the bicycles bump over the uneven road. Very occasionally one meets an ass-cart going to the village: sometimes one sees a few grouse taking their diet of stones off the road. Not many, though this is one of the few places where they drove grouse regularly in Ireland — the owner used to have 100-brace days before the war, and one can see the line of butts. It seems impossible that the shooting can be other than dull in such a dead flat, or that one can find running water. But we come to a stunted plantation, the road bends at right-angles to the left, turns again, and, just beyond the wood, there is the low grey bridge and the sparkling river deep in its high banks.

These high banks were one of the features, and the hazards, of our bog-stream. At long intervals it was cleared out by the Board of Works — deepened and straightened to prevent floods. After each clearance the banks became higher, and on the sides the grass and nettles and thistles, protected from the wind, grew high. So that, as one had to climb down the bank to get a proper approach to one's fish, there was great danger of disturbing them — and often, at the critical moment, one's fly got caught up in the high vegetation behind. The water was so dark that one could never see one's fish — one had to judge whether the rise was a four-pounder or a half-pounder. But whatever the size, each fish required a careful stalk and a lot of catching, for, apart from other dangers, the river became a mass of weeds as the summer went on, and these were of course never cut.

Needless to say, the percentage of losses was high. Once I hooked a great fish which took me into the weeds, at a place where the water was shallower, and one could see the sandy bottom. Hand lining was tried in vain, but the fish was still on and seemed firmly hooked. I put the rod down, took off all my clothes, and waded in, holding the rod in one hand and the line in the other, till I reached the fish. He seemed to me enormous, and he had twisted the cast round a branch stuck in the weeds. Reaching my hand down I broke the branch and he was free but still hooked. And still full of life, for he darted down-stream again, and I was left to get ashore and pursue him. Then might have been seen — if there had been any to see — the spectacle of a middle-aged gentleman, stark-naked, struggling through nettles and thistles, and over rocks and stubs, on a slippery bank with rod held high, shouting and roaring for help which never came from his companion deeply engaged far away. The fish went faster than the fisherman, got into the weeds again, and broke me. He won the battle as he deserved to do. More than ever did I rejoice, as I dried myself in the sun, in the solitude of the Silver River.

Maurice Headlam, *A Holiday Fisherman*

When we were clear of the little bay but still in shallow water, I asked where I was to begin fishing. Patsey's answer is among our classics. It came as a matter of course — 'Where you are, sir; fish away, there's tons of them below you.' I laughed and repeated the phrase in mocking disbelief. 'There's tons of them below you!' My scepticism hurt Patsey, but he bided his time. Two years later he took his kindly revenge. Again it was May, but later in the month. It was a warm and balmy evening with scarcely a breath of wind. Patsey had gone home, as I thought, and we were just finishing dinner when the maid came to me and whispered that Patsey was in the hall and wished to speak with me. When I joined him he was a trifle excited. 'Put on your coat, sir, and come in the boat; I have something to show you.' I protested that a dinner-jacket was hardly the costume for a fishing excursion, but as there was to be no fishing I put on the coat and went with him. It was a perfect spring night; the lake was a polished mirror reflecting the light of the moon, almost at the full. He pulled swiftly to the southern shore and paused. 'Listen, sir!' All about us were feeding fish — one circle flowing into the next; their 'chopping' could be heard distinctly and among them were some very heavy fish. They were feeding along the shore up to the very edge of the grass. Then away he pulled to one of the islands, halting in the shadow of the overhanging trees; chop, chop, chop; everywhere it was the same — under the overhanging bushes, at the ends of the oars, out in the deep as far as we could see. Then he carried me off to a shallow, rocky bay, and there it seemed as if all the trout in the lake were congregated — it was unbelievable! As we crossed the lake on the way home he paused again, in the deepest part, and as far as one could see there were feeding trout. Then he spoke and his voice was very serious. 'Do you remember, sir, the first day you were here? You were after asking me where you should fish, and I told you — "Where you are, there's tons of them below you" — you laughed at me, sir, and thought I was telling what wasn't true. Well, sir,' — and here he spoke with a new firmness — 'was I right?' Then I made the best apology I was able. He had been right, perfectly right. He had not overstated the facts by so much as a pound. When I had made my apology he merely said, 'Very good, sir' — and the boat sped back where the lights shone out from unshaded windows and the sound of the piano came sweetly across the stillness. I have believed all Patsey's stories from that moment.

F D Barker, *An Angler's Paradise*

Surgeon, antiquarian, scholar, writer, adulterer and father of Oscar Wilde, Sir William Wilde's The Beauties of the Boyne and Blackwater *celebrates two wonderful limestone rivers in County Meath.*

Among the many scenes of beauty and of interest with which this fair island abounds, we know of none which combines such variety of the former or so many objects of the latter as the *Pleasant Boyne.* And although this river does not burst upon us amidst the wild and stern grandeur of the mountains, with dashing torrent o'erleaping in its rapid course all the barriers of nature, or making its echoes heard among the deep hollows of dark-wooded dells, but pursues the quiet, even tenor of its way, through a flat but rich and fertile country, winding by "its own sweet will" through broad savannahs and by green inches, where the calm ripple of its placid waters disturbs not the song of the mavis; still it possesses charms and beauties, and that, too, without a rival in this or perhaps any other country. Slow, calm, and tranquil in its early course, the mower whets his scythe in the deep meadows by its brink, and the reaper gathers the corn from the very margin of its waters; the swift and martin skim over its clear surface, and the robin sings in the ancient thorn that rises out of the adjoining hedge-row. The very may-fly, as it lights upon it, breaks the mirror of its surface. The wide-spreading circles which mark the springing of the trout, or the timid breathing of the roach, are all, save the flapping of the water-hen, or the easy paddle of the baldcoot, that disturb its placid bosom.

In this gentle stream there is no inequality — no roar of waters nor spray of cataract; it is not boisterous nor yet sluggish; neither broken by the sudden rapid, nor calmed by spreading into the broad lake; but, pure and undefiled, it springs from the crystal fountain of the living rock, — its source sanctified by religious veneration, and commemorated in legend and in song; serene and peaceful, like a true philosopher, it glides noiselessly on, in deep but calm repose bestowing the blessings of fertility on the counties through which it flows; bearing on its bosom the inter-course which socializes man; enriching, beautifying, and civilizing, it receives in return the homage of its tributaries, and finally mingles with that eternity of waters, the sea.

Sir William Wilde, *The Beauties of the Boyne and Blackwater*

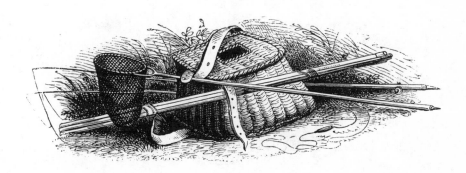

153

TROUT

Hangs, a fat gun-barrel,
deep under arched bridges
or slips like butter down
the throat of the river.

From depths smooth-skinned as plums
his muzzle gets bull's eye;
picks off grass-seed and moths
that vanish, torpedoed.

Where water unravels
over gravel-beds he
is fired from the shallows
white belly reporting

flat; darts like a tracer-
bullet back between stones
and is never burnt out.
A volley of cold blood

ramrodding the current.

Seamus Heaney, *Death of a Naturalist*

We wait and watch the sunset. These Lough Derg sunsets are indescribably glorious. The sun hangs low in the west — a great crimson ball swinging in ultra-marine deepening to darkest sapphire. He drops lower and lower, and his reflection streams across the black water — a broad pillar of fire. A cloud swims in front of him and the whole western sky is red, and the waters turn blood-colour, reminding us of the legend from which Lough Derg derives its name. And the mountains to the west stand out black as ebony, with a fringe of fire, and the eastern hills light up in the after-glow; and then the gorgeous spectacle fades away, and Danny shivers and says: "It's time to go home, sir!" So we go home; and no sound breaks the stillness of the night save the creaking of the thole-pins, and the gurgle of the yielding water at the bow, or the far-off lowing of the cattle on the Galway shore.

And then the grey seabirds come. They come from the east, and they go to the west. Why? No man knows. But they come, and float over us, following some inscrutable law of their own. They come from the east, they vanish in the west like wraiths; without a sound, without a trace — they are gone.

I think of them as the spirits of the many races that have lived and loved and warred and passed away over this mystic land. Fomorians, Milesians, Celts, Danes, Normans and Saxons — they have all left their traces here for those with eyes to see. We carry on our dapping — and this to me is almost its greatest attraction — in a region inconceivably rich in legendary lore: of Maeve, and Finn, and Oisín; of Bryan of Kincora, when he crushed the hosts of Asmond, and the Leinster men broke before the Dalcassian battle-axes. Of the wars of the Geraldines and the Butlers, of Confederates and Covenanters; and even still in the homes of the people they tell of Sarsfield and his irresistible dragoons. And so my story ends.

Next morning Danny and I exchange regretful but not hopeless farewells.

"Ye'll be back for the dapping next year, sir?"

"Please God, Danny. Good-bye."

He returns to his fruit trees and his flowers — and I to noise and smoke and civilisation!

Sir Thomas Grattan Esmonde, *Hunting Memories*

Cloon Lake lies high up in the mountains, yet not so high but that farther still from the sea is the Red Lake, above whose shore a steep cliff rises where the golden eagles had till some few years back their last breeding-place in Kerry. I have been there in my time, and have caught from the bank trout very unworthy of such impressive surroundings; but this year Cloon Lake was far enough and good enough for me. Ten miles from the little hotel, it is twenty from the nearest railway-station: and thank heaven, the road to it leads across a ford which effectually shuts out the motor-driving tourist.

There were four of us, two ladies and a tall lad who, despite much patient endeavour in English waters, had never compassed the capture of even a herring-sized trout. I passed my word that in Kerry he should catch more than we could eat; and on this day a gridiron was brought along with us, though the ladies were most doubtful of its finding use.

We had got the rods ready, one with a spoon bait up to troll for salmon, and before we launched the boat, "Patsy," I said, "did you put in the life-belts?" Patsy grinned at me reproachfully with his one front tooth. Last autumn I had made an earlier fishing raid to Cloon, and as we drifted down the lake shore, cheerfully employed in hooking and landing a succession of small trout, it became fairly evident that the boat was leaking. However that is nothing unusual on Irish lakes; but the breeze freshened and as we turned to row back from the end of the drift, she met the wave, and every dip of the oars drove her deeper into it and streams poured in from all the upper seams. I sat in the bow and bailed, while Patsy and Patsy's father, Micky, rowed; but the bailing did not lower the water in her, and my friend in the stern, W. S. Green, who knew as much about boats as any man living, called out that she was sinking. Neither of the boatmen could swim, and I thought myself very unlikely to reach the shore in boots; there were some very uncomfortable minutes while the oars tugged at that water-logged craft and I bailed frantically. But she kept afloat till just before we reached the bank, and as we scrambled on to an outlying rock, Micky observed very placidly; "You were right enough, sir, she was sinking."

"And what would you do if she sunk sooner, Micky?" I asked. "Walk out, sure," said Micky. "Sure I knew with the last five minutes there wasn't five foot of water in it." Patsy turned to his father in a rage. "You knew that. And me tearing the inside out of me rowing!"

That mishap had put the fear of God into Patsy, and he had the boat staunch enough this year; and as we began to troll, one of the ladies screamed out that "her rod was jumping". There was much exhortation and advice before the line could be reeled in, and when the cast came in view, not one trout but two were on it, and we landed them, set the flies fishing once more, and in a couple of minutes the rod "jumped" again, and again she had caught a couple. So it went on for the whole drift, and we had fully a dozen landed before an hour's fishing was over and it was time to think of luncheon on the island.

As we paddled up, there was a great turmoil in the trees and a grey crow flew off sullenly; a flutter of wide wings showed where a heron had been hunting the robber from her nest. But she left it with a croak and much flapping as we landed and made our way through the hollies with which the island is chiefly wooded: I climbed up and there were the two eggs, blue like a duck's, and about the same size. We ought to have found a duck's nest too, for one rose almost at our feet out of a tangle of undergrowth: but it was too cleverly hidden and we gave up the search to superintend Patsy's cooking.

He had lighted a fire by this time, an easy matter that dry day, and he was busy cleaning the trout with the help of my pocket-knife. But it would be unjust to Patsy if I left it to be supposed that he needed all conditions so favourable. There came another day when he and the schoolboy were out on another lake, with nothing but bread and trout for luncheon, and the rain came down in torrents. Patsy had only two matches, and no knife; but he had also the stump of a candle and a safety pin, and with these aids he prepared the trout and got a fire to cook them by. You never can tell what will come in useful on a day's fishing.

But at this first venture all was plain sailing, and soon the gridiron was laid on the glowing cinders and we all sat with our eyes centred on the trout that curled up as they grilled first on one side then on the other. On that day we affected to be civilized and ate them with pointed sticks of holly. Later, we dispensed with the sticks; but whether with fingers or with forks we found trout so cooked and so eaten delicious beyond expression — and a welcome change from the inevitable sandwich.

Finally, when we had well eaten, the boy went off with Patsy to renew the slaughter of trout, and the rest of us were content to be idle under shade of holly and arbutus, where a mossy rock sloped into the lake: and as we sat there quiet, the noises of the island life began to be heard about us, all the talk of birds. It soon revealed the presence of a second heron's nest with young birds in it, clamorous to be fed. They were the oddest pair that I saw when I scrambled up, three-parts fledged, beak complete of course, and menacing, in front of the bright yellow-ringed eye: the wing coverts were fairly furnished, and as I saw them at first crouching into a confused heap into the saucer of loose-piled sticks which is their nest, they seemed very tolerably plumaged. But presently when I moved nearer, both got awkwardly on to tall tottering legs and revealed the most indecorous lack of feathers about the rump. They staggered uneasily out to the extremest rim of the nest, and in terror that they would fling themselves out, I climbed down. But when I reported my find, needs must the birds be looked at; and having made arrangements to catch them if they jumped, I went up with a landing-net and got it over their heads. One I left, the other came down in the net's bag, quaintly entangled, and very droll when we got him out. That heron will never know how near he came to taking the journey to London in a railway-carriage; but a heron's personal habits are untidy and

I pointed at the state of the branches about the nest and that decided it — that and some uncertainty if the creature would live. I carried him back again and left for a peace-offering two trout in the nest, which may also have served to confirm to the old bird the young ones' story.

After that, we had decided to climb one of the surrounding mountains, and there was great cutting of hollysticks; but our way from the shore led past a cottage, and trusting to the traditions of the country, I went in and begged that tea might be ready for us when we came down. Thoughts of that tea acted perhaps as a drag, for the climb did not reach beyond the lower slopes: and lovely as the view was, the tea was lovelier. I never saw whiter linen than was spread for us, with good scones, with butter that had been in the churning when we passed up, and creamy milk and eggs enough to feed a regiment. We were glad to have a score or more of trout to leave in return for that cordial hospitality, and on our way down the lake we picked up perhaps another dozen to bring home.

It was late when we left, and passing almost into twilight from the golden close of day. She for whom chiefly I had planned the excursion turned round on the car as the horse started for his long trot down the narrow alarming little mountain road. "Oh, Cloon Lake" she cried back to the water, "you've been very good to us."

And that is the best of all the memories in this book of mine.

Stephen Gwynn, Duffer's Luck

It's a grand time in the Corrib country when the Mayfly starts to rise. From all over Ireland the anglers come in their hundreds, and from most parts of England too in the days of peace and sense and decent travel. Accommodation anywhere within sight of the lakes is at a premium and most of the fishermen have their rooms booked at Ashford and other hotels year after year, and are ready packed and waiting at home for the telegram that will be sent to them to say that the first Mayfly have taken to the air. You'll see hundreds of boats on Corrib at this season of the year, and hundreds of men, women and children all round the lake shores, armed with butterfly nets and ventilated collecting-boxes, chasing after the elusive Green-drake Mayfly which is considered best for dapping. The hatch usually rises at about eleven o'clock in the morning, and as soon as possible after that you'll see the flycatchers gathered on the lawns of Ashford and elsewhere, offering their fragile winged stock-in-trade to the impatient anglers, who are not at all particular what they pay so long as they are not delayed in their eager rush to the boats nor kept too long from their all-absorbing sport. For time is not to be wasted — the rise only lasts three weeks at most, and but ten short days of that period can be counted on for the real rigour of the game. It is a light sou'-westerly breeze they look for, these disciples of Walton, and given that, and a spot of luck, a pair of them will come in with thirty good trout between them against a day of excitement and hope and tantalising encounter. Fish that would never rise for an imitation fly, big wily experienced fellows up to fourteen pounds in weight, will cast caution and discretion to the four corners of the lake and take greedily the greenish-yellow lure that is dangled above them on the roof of their home. For, as Izaak Walton said: "They love the Mayfly, which is bred of the cod-worm or caddis."

And what a strange breeding it is to be sure. Hatched from eggs laid in the water, the larvae, predacious, hungry, and armed with formidable jaws, spend a long worm-like existence of twelve months in the lake, fighting for food, growing, changing, and casting the while maybe twenty coats or skins on the long road to perfection. And always striving towards that exciting exhilarating day when they may thrust up towards the light and the air and the sun, and burst their water-bound strait-jackets to take to the air on fragile wings, light as gossamer, the perfect imago at last. No thought of food then — no need for food — no means of eating it — for the Mayfly has no jaws and but the veriest rudiments of a mouth. Such mundane things were cast aside with those other vulgar trappings of a half-lit wormy world. What need of food anyway when the imago has but a few short hours to live — and less than that if the fly-catchers are about. Up, up, up into the sunlight, sick and crazy with love, up in that mad delirious nuptial flight, guerdon of their long dark months of striving. And with their mating done, and future generations assured, their new-found winged life so madly begun comes to a quick and sober end. But the eggs are already being laid and soon more larvae will commence their strange slow pilgrimage towards the light and the few intoxicating hours of life and love and air-borne frenzy.

A light bamboo rod is used for this Mayfly dapping, from fourteen to sixteen feet long according to fancy, and the special dapping hook is attached to this by means of a thin silk blow-line. Two Mayflies go to each hook, neatly impaled through their bodies at the wing junctions, and the secret of the art is to work with a touch as light as the bait itself — lightly — lightly — and never drenching your fly nor giving way to coarse handling when your victim takes. Easy does it now — easy and lightly. There he goes — and a big fellow too. Yerra man, don't strike yet or you'll lose him. Count one — two — three — and strike now. You have him, begob, and a fine bucko too. Ten pounds or I'm a Dutchman. Good man, me da! It's a great game, and whilst it lasts the excitement is intense. The whole countryside is transformed into one vast paradise of anglers, and you'll hear nothing else but talk of fish and breeze and light and water. And it's not only trout that are killed but many a good bottle of the wine of the country too, and that's no word of a lie. For it's a thirsty pastime this same dapping, and sure what's drink for anyway.

It all starts towards the end of the third week of May, and by the middle of June you wouldn't see a dapper in the world. But the grilse have come into the lake before then and sure they take the loneliness off it. And there's always August ahead, but it's Daddylonglegs and Grasshoppers we'll be dapping with then, and the fish rising for them nearly as eager as they were for the Mayfly itself.

Richard Hayward, *The Corrib Country*

BIG FISH

CHAPTER 6

Big fish — how magical the words are, how evocative of dreams, ambitions and occasional reality! But, while the majority must bide their lives without a true monster, there are those who succeed, just as there are those who hook and lose a great fish.

So here they are, the victors and the vanquished, sharing the extremes of joy and sorrow with us. Amongst the tales of the vanquished is Dick Grove Annesley's sixty-pounder lost on the Cummeragh stream of the Blackwater. And the victors? They, too, are here — Barker's great days on Inchicrag and, peerless as ever, Stephen Gwynn's matchless tale of a trout so big that it gave him forever 'the sway of Corrib'.

The most extravagant cruisers I ever met were on a river in Co. Louth, Ireland. In mayfly time the big fish — and they had been killed up to six pounds — would traverse regularly a beat which might be a hundred yards long. Invisible, a heavy trout would sail up and down this in sedate and leisurely fashion, devouring the mayflies he met on his road. Now such a world-traveller was in a different category from the stroller of the Test, whom you can reach without changing your place, merely by lengthening or shortening line. The Irish fish soon passed out of range; if you ran after him, you either found that you were usefully showing your fly to his tail, or else you put him down. The better plan, the one I was advised to adopt, was to choose some place about the middle of his beat, where there were no obstructions and the regular flow of the stream allowed your fly to float long without a drag. Once there, you noted the path through the stretch which he took on his journey up and down, a path which varied little, and you selected a spot where you could cast straight across to him. Then you knelt down when you saw his rises getting nearer and nearer, you waited till he was ten to fifteen yards off, then you cast, kept your fly floating to the last second, and then immediately cast again, so that your fly was on the water without an interval.

There are many exciting incidents in angling; a big fish splashing at sedge in the still dusk; a salmon of thirty pounds boiling at your fly; the last stage of the fight with a three-pounder on 4x gut, but I have rarely been more shaken than by one of these cruisers, whom I verily believe to have been five pounds. I had chosen my station cautiously and prudently; I studied his paths to an inch; I knew him to be sixty yards below me; then suddenly there he was, taking a mayfly, forty yards off. I waited what seemed an endless time. Had he passed me? The mayflies were drifting down in a string and I watched them idly. They were fifteen yards below — and he took all three, one above the other.

Quickly I cast; my fly floated two yards, I whipped it off before it dragged, and instantly put it on the water again, beautifully cocked. It had hardly sailed two inches when he had it; he had it with a gulp, but with my usual fatuity I missed him. I hit him hard, there was a boil like a submarine mine, and that five-pounder was seen no more.

J W Hills, *A Summer on the Test*

When the captain saw my flies, he offered to back the black and orange, and the orange fly, half-a-crown each, against the yellow heckle fly. I took him up on each. Kean whispered to me, "Sir, there is no click to your new wheel, and it runs smooth and silent, so let out a little more line, that your fly may be a little below the other." I did as directed, and caught two more large fish. We had now ten; when it was proposed to fish the next stream, a very rapid one, called Poul a Herra. Here I was obliged to take the second oar, but keeping my yellow heckle fly still near me.

We had made several turns, and could scarcely keep the boat against the stream, when my rod had a tremendous pull. I instantly shipped my oar, and found, from the weight and strength of the fish that he must be very large. We, as usual, went to shore, at the Clare side of the Shannon, and, after about twenty minutes' hard and fatiguing play, he showed enormous: he was a new run fish, not long in the river. I brought him within reach of the gaff, when Kean made an attempt at him, and only scraped his back; away then he went across. We were again obliged to take to the cot, and follow him to the other side, and bring him back again, the banks at the Limerick side being high, and it being highly dangerous to attempt to gaff him into the cot in deep water. We at length killed him. He weighed forty-eight and a half pounds, and was the largest salmon I ever killed, though I have hooked much larger. Captain Cotter, in the month of May following, killed, with a fly on three-twist gut, on the stream of Donass, a salmon fifty-nine pounds weight: he was turning a little brown, but was a splendid fish.

O'Gorman, *The Practice of Angling*

I think it must have been the next year that I went over to stay with Dick for Whitsuntide. We fished hard and did fairly well everywhere, except in Cummeragh stream, which always looked perfection, but was in fact extremely dour.

Then, one day something stirred up the fish and we got three in it all within an hour, and I rose what appeared to be a very big one. The river was not high, but there was a good flow, and after fishing Cummeragh all down with a prawn, Dick decided to try for the big one with a worm.

The moment he reached the spot where the fish had risen the line checked, and then began to run out with those surreptitious jerks which are so exciting and make self-control and patience so difficult. Dick gave him due time and the fish was fast. Obviously it was no small one, for with astounding ease he ran right up and stayed for some minutes in the neck of the stream where in those days thousands of gallons of water came shooting down from the pool above in a long smooth and glassy glide, while the line hummed with the vibration.

Then he turned heavily and slid swiftly into the stream, and, swimming deep, passed the slip of shingle on which we were standing. After taking a short turn round the eddy opposite, he ran down some eighty yards, this time more quickly, towards the very end of the stream. There, still unseen, he turned head up and remained stationary. We therefore waded down and out as far as we could to try to get some control by having the rod as much over the fish as possible. But at the first increase of pressure he began to drop down tail first towards the rougher water. This was most dangerous, for the rapids ended in a violent stream, known as the 'Whirls', where many a good fish has been lost. I waded out as deep as I dared below the fish and threw stones to prevent him going down, but without any effect. Very slowly he dropped down and down. The water was shallower; a quarter of the trace was showing. We were almost in the rapids now. Then he stopped again and remained stationary. He was not more than five yards away, but still invisible, and for five minutes nothing would move him up or down. Dick put on all the strain he could. Even the leads were now visible, twisting and trembling with the strain. I half thought of trying to gaff him where he lay. I think it might have been done, though the wading was very deep and rough, and the stream strong. Even today it gives me a twinge of regret that I did not — for suddenly his tail just showed for a moment above the surface — an immense tail, and incredibly far from the trace. He must have been well over four feet long, a super-fish! Then, with one rush of a hundred yards, he was off into the 'Whirlpool'. The line gave a twang and came flying back minus leads and hook — clean cut through. 'Gone!' ejaculated Dick with a gasp, 'and on a worm too,' and he slowly wound in the line.

That was, I am convinced, an unusually large fish, sixty pounds weight at least, judged by its length.

G D Luard, *Fishing Fortunes and Misfortunes*

I have been, once at least, in touch with a really big trout, and this is how it happened. There is a small lake that lies deep-set among steep, low hills, some two miles and more from the Grey House. It is a lonely spot, not an inhabited house within sight. At the lower end of the lake is a rugged crag from the summit of which rises an ancient tower, now a roofless ruin, heavily hung with ivy, the tenement of countless jackdaws. Another ruin — that of an ancient church with a crowded and disordered burial-ground about it — crowns one of the hills. A tiny beck winds down a grassy valley and enters the lake at the end opposite the tower.

In this dark and sombre lake there are trout in plenty and perch, but never a pike. Originally the trout were brought from Inchicrag, some seventy or eighty years ago, and have prospered. Plentiful though they are, to take them is no easy matter; indeed, there are days, and many of them as I know to my cost, when to fish here is as useless as to cast on the lawn. There is an exasperating unanimity about these fish. When the mood for fly possesses one the multitude is possessed; then, without rhyme or reason, down go the lot, and that's the end.

One bright sunny afternoon in May we walked across to see what an evening might afford us in the way of sport. We were early and we sat in the shade of the tower and talked fish until the sun dipped behind the hill. Even then we did not go out, but watched the fish feeding close in to the banks. It was getting pretty dark when at length we took to the boat. There was not enough breeze to move the light boat, and I was paddled along within easy casting of the shore. So many fish were feeding that it was puzzling to decide over which to cast; but we did very well and picked up nine nice fish of over a pound each. Here again I found the trout not in the least shy of the boat or of my casting — repeatedly they rose within a yard of the boat.

Then came a great excitement. Somewhere out in the deep and

the dark was a 'gobble' that made us both cry out. 'A whacker!' said Patsey. I fervently agreed. We went in search of that fish and, through the noise he made, were able roughly to locate him. He appeared to be moving about, working toward the middle of the lake, and apparently taking everything that came his way. Then began, I am ashamed to admit, some pretty hasty and bad casting. He was here, there and everywhere, except where my flies happened to be; but even my thrashing failed to frighten him. On he went, sucking in the flies with a noise that could be heard across the lake. I was at such a tension that when the 'knock' came, as it did, I struck 'fit to lift him', as Patsey said, with the inevitable result — away went the Monster, taking my upper bobber with him, and with him went the chance of a lifetime. Oh! the misery of that moment.

Patsey did his best to console me. 'Faith, it might happen to any one, sir, waiting so long. Many a time I did it myself, gave a welt and left the casting-line and all in a feller. 'Tis a pity, sir, a great pity, but it can't be helped.'

'Ah, Patsey, if only we didn't do stupid things! It *was* a big trout.'

'It was, sir, a very large trout; devil such a trout did I think was in the lake at all.'

We were still lamenting, when a fog came down suddenly and put an end to our fishing.

The next morning I took down my cast to repair the damage and found, sticking on the point of the middle fly, the scale of a trout. When I so madly struck that big fish the upper fly came away and the middle one tore across his back. How big the trout was you may say for yourself, you who have caught trout, when I tell you that the scale would cover the butt-end of an ordinary lead-pencil. Patsey says fifteen pounds; his brother, an experienced fisher and not *my* boatman, declares that no fifteen-pounder ever wore a scale of that size.

F D Barker, *An Angler's Paradise*

It is given to few anglers to catch a monster trout. Stephen Gwynn was one and in this memorable encounter, he evokes all the anxieties, fears and triumphs of an unforgettable battle.

We are all of us anxious for the credit of our counties, but it has to be allowed that trout-fishing in Donegal means catching herring-sized fish. Ever since I began to use a rod, I have been seeing brown trout caught there, and till I was forty I could count on the fingers of my hands all the fish among them that turned a pound. But also, ever since I began to hear fishing stories (and to tell them), I had been hearing of the Big Trout — three pounds, five pounds, and so on up to any reasonable figure — hearing but not seeing; he was still "a hope, a joy, still longed for, never seen." Literally, until I began to fish Sessiagh lake in 1904, I had never set eyes on a brown trout of even two pounds. There, however, I met them, and then, I saw and (through sheer stupidity) lost a really big trout.

One thing, however, had resulted. The Big Trout of fiction had ceased to be mythical for me, and had become an object of pursuit. But, however ardently I hunted him in Donegal, with spinning-bait and with fly, I never approached the one I had lost, never could even pass the four-pound limit.

Perhaps providence thought of my disappointment and my perseverance; perhaps, as an Irish proverb says, "A fool does be lucky". Certainly I felt fool enough for anything when, in the end of August 1906, I unpacked my rod-case at Cong, preparing for my first day on Lough Corrib. A hurried journey to Galway had suggested the possibility of this fishing, and I came away with no time to examine gear, and by consequence was confronted with the fact that all my spinning-tackle was forgotten. I had nothing to show to my boatman, Lydon, except a green and silver wagtail minnow which his namesake, the tackle-maker in Galway, had persuaded me to buy — may providence reward him! For a companion bait, a spinner for the natural minnow was soon rigged, roughly but effectively; a couple of swivels which I chanced to have were let into a strong casting-line; and then, by Lydon's advice, we repaired to the local draper's shop, where it appeared other swivels could be got. They had no detached swivels, but offered me a very light spinning-trace, which after some discussion we decided to fish with as it was; and so equipped we started.

Even on that bleak ugly day of northerly wind and colourless skies the upper end of Corrib showed a fair challenge to Killarney. Thickly strewn with wooded islands, it is backed by ranges of bold mountain; but its chief charm lies in the romantic suggestion of the pass towards Maam, where its winding water, lost to sight between the cliff-like hills, tempts one to row continually onwards and explore what recesses may be enfolded among the gaunt crags that guard the entrance to the Joyces' country. This day, however, we were due to lunch near Lord Ardilaun's fine house and famous woodcock covers, and so we dodged and wheeled about round rocks and islands, aiming at the points where deep water fringes a shallow, and the big trout and pike cruise about looking for incautious fry.

Meanwhile, naturally, we talked about big trout; and it appeared that Tom Lydon had captured the show fish of the hotel, which, glossy in its glass case, had impressed me solemnly while I breakfasted. It weighed twelve pounds, he told me; and after it was sent to be stuffed he caught another half as big again. This fish, eighteen pounds, took a bait attached to a hand-line, and, as Lydon said, you could do nothing but throw the reel at him. It, being wooden, floated, of course, and the fish was eventually landed.

I listened as to a chapter of mythology, and in the meantime nothing happened. At last we turned homewards to lunch, and shortly after there was a pull at the rod from which the wagtail was fishing; but this first fish proved to be only an inconsiderable pike. It broke the ice, though: five minutes later there came a savage pluck at the same line, and the moment I had the rod in hand I knew we were into something heavy. Probably another pike, I thought, and sighed for waters where a big fish can be relied on to be a good fish. But at the next instant the unknown quantity made a short run — luckily crosswise, for his first race had nearly stripped my reel — and then floundered head and tail up. At all events, here was no pike; the sickly yellow gleam did not show itself. I set him down for a salmon long up and discoloured, and the boatmen found confirmation in the fact that he was now moving constantly up-wind. We got the boat parallel with him, and I shortened line as quickly as I could, while Lydon exhorted me to handle him gently, for he was on the light trace. We are accustomed to fish very light in the north of Ireland, and the mere thinness of the gut would not have terrified me; but when I thought of the local draper's shop, grave doubts — which I retract and apologise for — rose up in my mind.

Then suddenly, perhaps thirty yards off, the fish rose so high in the water that we could see him plainly; and his broad golden side was covered with huge black spots. Young Lydon shouted: "It's no salmon; it's a splendid great trout!" But his father was more eloquent. Dropping his oar, he shifted his place to the bow. "Maybe you'd better take the gaff," he said to the son. I felt then that this was indeed a great occasion, when this hardy veteran would admit the advantage of youth; and, Heavens above! how I wished that we had put our swivels into gut which commanded my confidence.

There are few incidents in the business of wearing down a heavy fish in a lake with light rod and tackle, but the strain on one's nerves is considerable when the prize is so uncommon as we knew this fish to be. Somewhere about ten pounds, I guessed him — at any rate, a bigger brown trout than my wildest ambitions had ever aspired to; and, contrary to all precedent, the nearer he came, the bigger he looked.

"He's fourteen pounds!" Johnny Lydon cried, when a great back showed for a moment above the water. Inwardly I set this down for exaggeration, but it added to my excitement that I had never seen experienced boatmen so eager and anxious. There was a continual fire of snapping injunctions from one to the other — generally speaking, instructions to do the thing which the man instructed had already begun to do. The boat in reality, and not I, was playing the fish; my part was only to keep an equable strain and watch that the reel kept absolutely clear.

We had come about half a mile with the fish, humouring him away from all dangerous possibilities of weed or rocky shallow; and another boat near by had stopped fishing and pulled over to watch the event. We were all anxious; but luckily the old grilse-rod's top was very limber, and I could be tolerably secure that no sudden plunge would meet with too much resistance. With an ordinary spinning-rod and that trace the odds would have been on the fish; and as it was, the tackle was wholly too light to lift his head. Gradually, however, and most skilfully, the boat was sidled down; I had learnt enough not to try to drag or force the fish, but rather to go to him. Still he kept sheering off from the side of the boat; and suddenly Johnny Lydon passed me and took up his position in the stern. It was an awful moment, for as he leant over he hid the line from me, and every angler knows that the eye, quicker even than the hand, tells when to ease off the strain and stop a heavy fish from floundering on the top of the water. But right or wrong, I left Lydon his own way, and kept up the strain through seconds that were like minutes, while he shouted his directions and the boat was backed quietly down.

One felt rather than saw when he actually struck; and he had reached out so far that he paused for an instant to recover, while the trout hung over the water on the gaff. Another lift, and it was in the boat at last. Lydon held it between his knees while he lifted an iron thole-pin for a "priest," gave a couple of decisive taps, and then laid it on the boards of the boat. If he was big in the water, he looked bigger now, for all of us gasped. "Fifteen pounds," I said. But the other boat drew over now and hailed us, and we did not venture to commit ourselves beyond thirteen or fourteen. This angler had scales, and lent them; and the pointer hung somewhere between sixteen and eighteen, as nearly as possible midway. It was a great moment. I never saw another fish weigh so much heavier than he was guessed at. The exact figure when we got him on kitchen scales was 16¾ lb. — and I quoted it to some one the same evening. But Johnny Lydon looked at me with pained eyes. "Sir, for the love of God, say seventeen pound." And for the love at all events of Johnny Lydon, I have always used the nearest round figure to the truth. How many anglers can say as much?

That was my first trout on Corrib. Lydon of Galway told me he had seen one killed a pound heavier, and my boatman, as I have said, also had an eighteen-pounder to his credit; but these things happened a good while ago, and my piece of luck was portentous. There is, of course, no question of skill in trailing a line behind a boat; and if it is true that in playing a salmon from the bank much depends on the gaffer, the same is far more emphatically to be said in the case of lake-angling. This fish, as we happened to be able to determine, took from fifteen to twenty minutes to kill, and he was gaffed before I ever got him on his side at all. With a less competent boatman I have been kept nearly an hour in killing a ten-pound salmon on tackle very little lighter. Consequently, it seems that we all had good reason to be pleased with one another, and certainly we were.

The rest of my day's fishing is of no interest. I killed altogether six fish — three trout (making twenty pounds), two small pike, and a large cannibal perch which took the minnow. But the history of the big fish has ramifications. It was decided that he should be stuffed, and accordingly, when we went in to lunch at my friend's house on the lake, careful preparations were made to send him off, and the fish reached Cong that afternoon in a well-secured box. We arrived not long after from the lake, and young Lydon announced the capture to the factotum of the hotel. He smiled pleasantly, and said, "May be!" Lydon grew eloquent and indignant, but I suggested that the hotel-keeper should go down to the post-office and heft the box. The proposal was scouted; of course he believed me implicitly. I went upstairs to my room, and approached the window in time to see this convinced person hot-foot to the post-office. He came back in a wholly altered frame of mind, eager now for measurements. I gave them him: length, thirty-three and a half inches, by nineteen and a half inches girth, and the girth almost uniform over the whole body of the fish, which was extraordinarily deep behind the dorsal fin. But if I had been wise, or he had been wise, he would have had the box opened, and had a public display in the street of Cong. For on the next day we were on Lough Mask and told our story there, only to be treated with the bare civility that is accorded to extravagant liars; and we returned to find word had reached the fourteen anglers fishing near by from Clonbur, and that all fourteen had refused to believe because none of their informants had seen the fish.

On the day following I departed, but a month later again passed through Cong. My carman met me some miles out, and at once launched out in copious Gaelic. "There was not the like of such talk in Ireland as was on your trout. Arrah, why did you bring him to Cong in a box? — and me getting my head broke over all the country!" Last Wednesday, he went on to explain, he had been in Ballinrobe, "and says one of the boatmen to me, 'No such a trout was ever caught in Corrib.' 'You're a liar!' says I to him; 'I seen it.' An' with that he struck me. An' sure, sir, I never seen it at all; only, what was I to say?"

He quoted to me also the opinion of a certain captain. "'Where is the man you say caught him?' says the Captain to me. 'Gone,' says I. 'And it was Saturday you say he caught him, and this is Thursday. Don't tell me,' says he. 'A man that caught a fish like that would fish a month for the comrade.'"

So it is to be feared that my fish, although quite authentic, is somehow clouded in myth at the place of his capture. Moreover, desire for the Big Trout is now extinct in me, since there is no reasonable probability of my catching one bigger; and, given my choice between the fly on a free-rising stream or lake, and the chance of heavy fish to be got by trolling, I shall henceforth always make for the place where there is less glory perhaps but more fun going. I trolled a blank day at my last visit to Cong, and it left me very disconsolate. But at my departure the carman consoled me with a magnificent phrase: "No matter, sir; you have the sway of Corrib!" That is the advantage of driving with a man who translates his thought from Gaelic. The phrase rose up in my mind when I walked one day this year into the shop where my fish was stuffed, and found two men in natural exultation over a twelve-pounder from the same lake. The stuffer turned to me: "It's a poor fish beside the one you got," he said. I felt for the man who suffered by the odious comparison, but it was something to be reminded that I had still "the sway of Corrib."

Stephen Gwynn, *Duffer's Luck*

FISH AT FINLOUGH

Finlough on the lovely Delphi fishery in County Mayo, and Kingsmill Moore stuck in a big seatrout. The 'Noll' who landed the trout was Oliver Gogarty, SC, son of the noted Irish man of letters, Oliver St. John Gogarty.

Finlough gave me my best sea trout, a fish of rather over six pounds, firmly hooked at the base of the dorsal fin. Over a fish so hooked there is little control. He is not in the least incommoded and there is no bit in his mouth with which to steer him. The moment after he was hooked he made upwind on a forty yard dash. Sea trout, unlike salmon, do not allow you a few seconds to collect your wits and a big sea trout runs faster than any salmon. Having finished his burst he turned broadside on and rested. A trout rod or even a salmon rod cannot drag a large fish, hooked halfway between head and tail, broadside through the water. The correct tactics are to row up wind of the fish and drift down, taking in line as you go. That fish would have no such nonsense. Every time the boat drew level with him he was off in another up-wind dash, again to rest broadside on. As he tired from running the spurts grew shorter, but he was still able to put himself up-wind and lie there recuperating. It became clear that he would have to be netted from his down-wind side. At last it was done. The boatman stole the boat up to him while Noll crouched in the extreme bow. There he was, still broadside on, about a foot under water. I held as hard as I dared. The boatman ceased rowing and Noll standing up and stretching out till he looked bound to fall in, slipped the long handled net under him, drew him nearer and lifted him in. That was the toughest fight I had with any fish, trout or salmon. No doubt a purist would have put that fish back, for he was foul hooked. I did not.

T H Kingsmill Moore, *A Man May Fish*

Some of the very big trout are quite beyond any of our lures. One very calm and sunny afternoon Patsey and I were strolling by the upper river, watching the trout in the clear water. There were plenty and some amongst them were fine fish. At one spot, where the stream narrowed through heavy weed-beds, there were no trout to be seen. I thought that suspicious, and said so. Patsey agreed, 'Faith, there'll be a smart stump of a jack hereabouts watching the run and we'll get him out of it, bad luck to him!' We searched until, under an overhanging bank, I made out the wave of a broad tail; then I caught sight of a fin, and the distance between the tail and the fin suggested a very respectable pike rather than a jack. 'He doesn't stand like a pike, Patsey.' ''Tis true for you, sir — 'tis his head we should be seeing, not his tail at all.' 'It can't be anything else; salmon can never mount the ladder at the mill?' 'They cannot, sir.' He stooped and shaded his eyes from the sun — ''Tis a trout, sir — a very large trout, one of those cannibal fellows. Faith, he's as bad in a stream as any pike; there he'll stand and devil a fish will pass him.' For three years that cannibal was to be found at that spot. All our attempts to lure him to his death failed, though he would have a look at them all; a small trout bearing a triangle so as not to prevent him swimming appeared to give him the most entertainment. But his career was mysteriously ended at last, much to the benefit of the river. He weighed, I understand, sixteen pounds, but was a poor fish.

F D Barker, *An Angler's Paradise*

On my first visit to Antrim, I had a very natural wish to see what the lake produced, and called on a professional for information, who promised to gratify my curiosity as soon as he could. Late one evening he came — it was after dinner, and a pullan had formed part of it, which fish you should know bears a very drowsy reputation. Now whether it was that fresh-water herring or a twenty-mile walk, I cannot undertake to determine, but certainly no young gentleman was ever more awfully sleepy. Hardly awake when we reached the cottage, I yawned out "Where is *the* trout?" "Your honour is standing on the same." The floor was thickly covered with flags and rushes, which, when partially removed, showed a sight that made me broad awake in a moment. *There* were fish of 4 lb., 8 lb., 12 lb., 15 lb. in dozens and dozens. That night my nervous system received a shock so severe, that I did not get over it for a week. How plainly that night comes back to me now! A thin stripling — the farthing candle — my poor comrade — the wretched hut — the flags and rushes — the dead bodies laid out in decent order, like heroes after a "stricken field" — you must admit the sight was very touching.

Not being anxious to gain a reputation for "tall talking," it is right to say that at this time I was not a very correct judge of weight; besides, my head was off, and the light bad. Nevertheless, I remember *perfectly* my companion telling me that in the previous season a trout weighing 31 lb. had been sent as an offering to Shunes Castle. It is hardly necessary to say this nice little lot had been netted for the Belfast market.

W Peard, *A Year of Liberty*

Here is G D Luard in unfamiliar surroundings, away from the Cork Blackwater and fishing instead on Lough Ennell (Belvedere) near Mullingar, County Westmeath, during the Mayfly.

It was my last chance, and I determined to make the most of it. My boat-boy had an awful cold, but I dug him out of his bed, and finding him fairly well I kept him at it from eleven till ten without a break! It was lovely on the water, with a warm breeze from the south, so it did him no harm. Yet though all looked favourable, it was a disappointing day, only a moderate fish or two, and but few rises to the dap. As the day advanced the breeze fell more and more and with its fall my hopes rose. It turned out a lovely evening, and by 7.30 practically a dead calm, so we made our way to the spot where we had seen the fish previously. Sure enough they began to rise, and earlier than usual, and they were big fish too.

The first I spotted was greedily taking spent gnats in a small circle about fifty yards away. My dry-fly rod was all ready, line greased, and spent gnat oiled.

The boy, who had become much more skilful, backed the boat towards him. Fifteen yards away, I made him stop the boat; the fish had ceased rising and I was afraid we should run over him. No, there he was again, poking up his big nose and gulping flies as fast as he could. Four times I covered what I expected to be the spot where he would rise next, without success. The fifth time I anticipated his movements aright, and after my fly had sat on the water for a few moments, during which my heart beat fast, there was a sploshing heave, the fly disappeared. I struck — no contact — fish put down. Damn!

By this time a good number of fish were rising in the rosy opalescent calm, but they were far more restless than the first. Several we hunted for two hundred yards or more without any success. Then one rose fairly near the boat. Three times he rose

— three times I cast and three times he changed direction; but the fourth time up he came and missed the fly altogether — another damn! The tension of this trout-hunting is so thrilling as to be almost intolerable.

Two or three more we pursued unavailingly and then another big fish took the fly beautifully — I have him — no! gone! Damn! too slow. Why did I forget to re-grease my line? Then two big fish began to rise steadily about thirty yards away, on each side of the boat. These were travelling more slowly than the others and moving definitely in the direction of a large island. They obviously meant business. I elected to pursue the left-hand one while keeping an eye on the other. He, or rather she, rose about every ten yards, and I covered her several times, but to no purpose.

At last my quarry reached the island shallows, with us some fifteen yards away, and turning along right-handed, proceeded to suck in flies at yard intervals. Over and over again I cast, but there were so many spent gnats that mine went unobserved. Then she turned back upon the same course, and seeing a spot where but few flies were collected, I put my fly on to it. Two more naturals she took in leisurely fashion, then strolled up and sucked mine in.

There was no mistake this time. I knew it was a good fish, and the weight and strength on my little rod were unmistakeable.

Twice she circled the boat, and then realizing the situation, set off towards deeper water with us following, which suited me better owing to the danger of the sharp edges of submerged limestone rocks.

A good fighter, she kept deep, any pressure on my part being answered by deep runs, and several times there was an unpleasant twang from the fish's tail, and once a dangerous scraping sensation, obviously a rock deep down.

At last, however, after some twenty minues, by which time my arm was getting quite tired, the fish began to weary, and her tail showed several times above the surface. Nearer and nearer I brought her, the boy carefully put out the net, the fish saw it and made a deep dive. I was astonished at her strength and resistance. I could see her far down standing on her head, and the effort to bring her up again was far greater than I expected. Up she came at last, however, and this time too weary to resist further. The boy gently put the net under her. For a moment her great length was balanced precariously, then she slipped in and was safely brought aboard. The boy was astonished at her size. I saw at once that it was a female fish. She was beautifully shaped, thick and short with a small head and big shoulders; of a lovely steel and blue shade and with quantities of rich black spots. I estimated the weight at something over five pounds, and eventually she proved to weigh 5 lb. 7 oz. The biggest trout I had yet caught.

It was now getting dark, the second fish had ceased to rise, and we made our way home, thankful that my last day had been kind and that I should return home with a real West Meath trout and sufficient of those feelings of triumph and unreasoning pride that always form such a satisfactory conclusion of an angler's holiday.

G D Luard, *Fishing Fortunes and Misfortunes*

GOOD DAYS AND BAD DAYS

CHAPTER 7

Every angler knows them — the days when all is at odds with
the world, when nothing is right, when fish are lost, when the
very day seems turned against one. Thus Maurice Headlam
laments never catching the Pig, Kingsmill Moore bungles it on
Belvedere, and Viscount Grey finds frustration and few fish on
the difficult waters of the Tipperary Suir.

But there are good days too. We have all had them. Few
however, can equal the astonishing fishing of Alington, who
caught a hundred two-pound trout in a fortnight. And where
today would we find the equal of the fishing enjoyed by Patsey
on 'Inchicrag' — or indeed that on the flooded Boyne, once
greatest of salmon rivers?

But it is all part of fishing. When times are hard, we may steel
ourselves and think *il n'est jamais plus tard que minuit*. And the
golden moments do come, to sustain us when it is indeed our
darkest hour.

The Erne is — was — a big, powerful river. Here is a close shave on its dangerous waters.

Of all the narrow squeaks that ever befell me in angling, about the worst was one which happened yesterday. I had been fishing our big river that was running two feet above its ordinary height, and the water was somewhat too dark for fly, except upon the shallows, where a big Jock Scot or a black and gold of the largest size sometimes scored. Truth to tell, we had for several days previously been reduced to the use of big spoons and silver Devon minnows in the bog-coloured water, and had met with but little success.

On the morning of which I am now writing I found myself some half-dozen miles down stream, below my quarters, paddling upwards a small canoe against a powerful current, and trailing a gold spoon from a short salmon-rod, in the wake of the boat. Now I am by no means an expert canoeist, and it soon became apparent to me that I had quite as much as I could do to get the crazy little craft along, without the dead pull of that long line and big spoon over the stern. Just as I was on the point of banking her, to wind up the tackle, there was a tremendous pull on the bait, and the winch flew round at a wild rate. The nose of the canoe was at once grounded, the paddle dropped, and the rod got into fighting position; but the fish had, meantime, shot across to the opposite side of the river, with a hundred yards of line out. Pressing him all that one could safely, some of the bellied line was recovered, and then it became apparent that the fish had found shelter in a leaf-covered branch, about six feet long, that had come down with the flood and got stranded. What was I to do? You cannot paddle a canoe and handle a salmon-rod at one and the same time; and after debating the "pros" and "cons" for some minutes, I decided to push off the little canoe and wind her across stream by the salmon-winch. It appeared feasible to me at the time, because the line was firmly fixed on the opposite side, and my utmost strength had failed to move the branch to which it was fast. Of course I assumed that the salmon was gone, and that the big spoon had got securely anchored. But my plan did not work out satisfactorily, for no sooner was the boat in the swift current, than she was swept down stream, the strain on the line dragged the branch afloat, and away the whole lot went towards the weir, barely two hundred yards below us! The next few seconds were about as exciting as could well be imagined; for the rod had gone overboard, and was hanging over the side, attached by a lanyard round my waist, and I was paddling frantically for the bank. The nose of the little craft grounded not twenty yards short of the dreaded weir. In less time than it takes to write this description I was on "terra firma," with the rod up, and rushing round below the fall to see what had become of that wretched branch. There was the horrid thing, bobbing about close up to the wall of the weir, at times floating out two or three yards, and then being drawn back by the under suction of that seething water. Winding in the line, every inch of which had been run off my reel, I put a steady strain on the offending bough, and eventually got it away down stream. In a shallow shelving bay the bough was stranded, and then, to my great astonishment, I discovered that the salmon was still on! He had got two turns of the treble spinning-trace round a springy branch, which had yielded to his struggles and prevented him getting a direct pull. The salmon was quite dead, and he proved to be a nice bright fish of fifteen pounds, with the sea lice on him. As I had done quite enough boating for one morning, the canoe was hauled up, I tramped home, carrying the rod and fish and all the way it kept running through my head that something very like a fluke had saved me from losing the number of my mess.

G W Gedney, *Fishing Holidays*

THE PIG

Maurice Headlam, an official with the British Government in Ireland in the early years of this century, loved Ireland and its sporting facilities. Alas the Louth Dee, where he stalks the great fish known as 'The Pig', is but a shadow of its former glory.

As soon as we heard that the Mayfly was up, those of us who knew left our proper occupations and made for Brophy's Hotel, where Willie, the best of the local fishermen, generally met us to tell us of the big fish. "I seen the Whale, sorr, him below the Thorn tree, and thim ye call Jones Major and Jones Minor along the straight, and the Pig and all. 'Tis a grand lot of fly we have this year," and so on: all the fish had names given by us and Willie adopted them. What is more, he seemed to be able to catch more than we did. He said he only used the artificial fly, like us, and perhaps he spoke the truth. Willie was a sportsman himself and may have resisted the temptation to use the deadly cross-line with droppers carrying natural Mayflies, which was the local way of fishing. And, as he was the leading local Sinn Féiner (in those days Sinn Féin was not taken seriously), perhaps he prevented the other local fishermen from using it.

The Pig was my pet antagonist. He was so called because he rolled in the water, like a fat pig, when taking his flies. I usually fished for him from the opposite side, for it was easier casting and there was a chance of getting Jones Minor, whose beat came up to the Pig's. Our method of fishing, developed after my experience at Richardstown, was to grease the line and oil the fly well, and then wait till one saw a great nose break the water down-stream. One knew it would appear again and take another fly, about ten yards higher up. So, as soon as the nose in the distance was seen, the fly was cast into the middle of the stream opposite with plenty of loose line, and one hoped that when the fish reached one's fly he would take it instead of the natural Mayflies that were always slowly drifting with the sluggish current. If he did, one of two things happened. If one had the self-restraint to wait till the fish had swallowed the fly, there was a fierce pull, a mad rush down, deep down into the weeds, and a sickening scrape against the thick stems deep below the surface. Then the cast came back, or some of it, without the fly. If one struck too soon, which was usually the case, there was a wild lashing on the top of the water and one's fly flew up and fixed itself in the branches of one of the "Sally" trees overhanging the stream. Often had I tried for the Pig and once I had scratched him in this way. Willie had hooked him once, he said, and lost him.

One year it occurred to me to try for the Pig from the near side of the river. On this side there was a dry ditch under a big willow tree about half-way up his beat. From this ditch it was just possible to get the fly on to the water, not casting overhead, for the boughs were too near, but with a sort of underhand switch, as nearly parallel with the ground as might be. There was just room between the willow tree and the next pollard to bring it off, but the high bank and the thick vegetation made it very difficult.

When, after tea, I had fixed myself uncomfortably squatting in the ditch, the Pig was feeding steadily and noisily. How hot I got, drying the fly in that narrow space, catching up perpetually in the sedges and bushes behind, climbing out cautiously (when the Pig had passed) on all fours to undo the fly. Casting again, lifting the fly gingerly when it began to get water-logged, repeating the whole process: while the Pig rolled up and down, snapping at the natural Mayflies but leaving mine untouched.

In daylight all our friends were wary enough and we had to fish with fine gut. But as it grew dark one used to change and put on a sea-trout cast — though it was not advisable to do this too early as it was apt to put them down. On this evening I was so excited that I forgot to change my cast as the light failed. It was my undoing. About 9 o'clock the Pig made a mistake and took my fly. There was a tremendous pull, the Pig jumped six feet (it seemed to me) in the air. I saw a bar of gold a yard long fly above the lower branches of the "Sally" tree and fall through them with a resounding smack into the water — and that was the last I ever saw of the Pig.

I was down the next week-end and met Willie, who had a twinkle in his eye. He said in his soft Louth burr, so like Northumberland — is the Danish blood responsible for the likeness? — "I cot the Pig, sorr — he weighed six and a half pound."

I know that I shall never see Ardee again, and that if I did I should be no better able to cope with those great trout — if they are there. Perhaps the new Irish Nation has bombed them all away, and probably there was no other method of making sure of them. But always memory calls up the tall, gaunt Workhouse of Ardee, by which we passed on the way to the river. At irrelevant times it comes before my eyes — when I am shaving, at a dinner-party, at a committee meeting. Then I smell again the peat smoke from the last houses of the little town. I see the broad high-road thick with white limestone dust and the turning of the little stony boreen under the Workhouse wall by which one reaches the river, and the boggy meadow between the river and the Workhouse. I see again the Mayflies drifting slowly on the dark water, the bubbles left where a trout has gulped one down, my rod point wavering as my hands tremble with excitement while I watch the great nose poking up in leisurely progress towards my waiting fly. And all the while I am conscious that behind me, in the cold, grey light of an Irish May evening, there stands, watching sarcastic and aloof, the grey mass of the Workhouse of Ardee.

Maurice Headlam, *A Holiday Fisherman*

One day at Derravaragh early in May 1972, before the Mayfly was up (on an average year around the 19th), I saw the top trout man Cecil Gibson all tacked up and ready to go. Asking him if he had a spare twine (excuse) to start my Seagull, he offered to take me with him as his friend had not turned up. This trip turned out to be the most wonderful experience of my life on a lake.

The knowledge he had accumulated over a lifetime of fishing mostly on his beloved Derravaragh was told to me with obvious pleasure. His stories of the good old days before the OPW devastated the Inny (which flows in and out of Derravaragh) were marvellous. He was the first person to tell me the most closely-guarded secret of those years — when to fish the calm lanes where trout cruise, nymphing on insects unable to break the surface tension and when to give your attention to the sud lanes when different breeds of fly are hatching. It was his opinion at the time (and how right he was) that Derravaragh was on the way out. He could see the signs going up all over the lake but nobody would listen to him. "Fishing is good today, so what?" was the attitude.

We were not long out of Donore towards Meehans when he boated his first trout of about 1.5 lbs which he returned to the water. Seeing how surprised I was, he said "this is a great fishing day and the wind is blowing from the Raa Shore, I hope to catch my bag limit of larger ones than that." He caught over twenty trout. When he had five "kept" he really shocked me by the size of trout he was releasing waiting for a big one.

He got the one he was waiting for which brought his bag limit to 6 weighing from 2.25 to 5.25 lbs. He then turned all his attention to me, taking my three flies off and replacing them with three of his own. I had two trout caught at this time, neither of 2 lbs. He showed me the angle to cast at and the correct speed to draw the flies in, which is dictated by the wind and the speed the boat is drifting at. In just over an hour I had my bag limit, one of 4.25 lbs.

There was a partition with swing doors in the local pub where he drank after a session on the lake. Cecil's car would pull up outside, and by the time he reached the front bar, the doors were swinging — the local anglers had scrammed down to the back bar. Very rarely could they match his catch. He was top man O.K.

There is an inscription on a rock at the weigh-in at Donore which reads *Cecil Gibson 1919 to 1979*, recording the number of years he was a member of the Derravaragh Trout Protection Association. It is just as well he has left his beloved Derravaragh. If he were alive now to see the sorry state it is in, it would break his heart.

Jim Reynolds, *A Life by the Boyne*

BUNGLING ON BELVEDERE

I had been asked to a supper picnic on Lough Belvedere, and my host suggested that we might bring our rods on the off chance of finding a fish cruising for Silverhorns under the trees which line so much of the shore. Not very hopefully — it was August and the rise to the big sedges should have been over — I put a box of dry flies in my pocket. There was, I knew, a cast in the lid but I had forgotten that the cast had been made up for small Slaney trout and was 2x tapered to 4x.

No trout were rising under the trees so we rowed out to an island for supper and sat on gossiping while the sun sank below the horizon. Just as it did so my host pointed to a patch of the lake about a quarter of a mile away and said, "What on earth is that?" I looked. In a small area not more than three hundred yards square the trout were wallowing like pigs. In the rush, I had not even the sense to cut away the finer portions of my cast. When we arrived at the area of activity (it had shifted several hundred yards further away while we made our preparations) we found it criss-crossed in every direction by the lines of immense fish swimming under water, coming up now and then to slash at the scuttering sedges. Trout often take a moving sedge with a bang. These trout took like runaway railway trains. I was broken four times in rapid succession by fish not one of which looked to be under five pounds. When I tried to fish with a free reel the barb of the big hook did not go home and the fish kicked off. Still I never thought of cutting down my cast to the three feet which would have been quite sufficient in the growing dark. My companion, with a strong cast, was broken at least once but got a fish of over four pounds, while I did not land a single one. It was a quite ghastly bit of bungling.

T H Kingsmill Moore, *A Man May Fish*

Lough Owel bears little resemblance to her sisters, being surrounded by shores far more bold, broken, and bare. Lying in a vast rocky basin, composed probably of limestone, its clearness and purity are remarkable. Over its entire surface myriads of bubbles rise from unknown springs, and, in fact, the lake is one vast fountain of delicious water. This, combined probably with the clean bottom, gives the trout the peculiarly silvery character that distinguishes them from all others with which I am acquainted. We found our boat drawn up on the south-east corner, near a circular fairylike island, planted with larch and flowering shrubs, and, launching, pulled for the western side, in order to make our first drift towards a high headland on the opposite side. Lough Owel was a special favourite with Willie, being, as he said, "a place where a fish in earnest might be killed," so I gave him a day; nor was it long before his line was sailing gracefully, far in advance of our humble bark. Here and there, at long intervals, the small circling eddy of some rising fish was seen as we glided on; but nothing came in our way till within two or three hundred yards of the rocky shore, when a trout sailed up, dexterously sucked off my fly, and disappeared. There was a momentary glimpse of a very broad tail. "Out with the paddles, and over him again!" but before the words were uttered, the folly of the order became apparent. The first dip of the oar would have driven the fish from his ground, so the boat was allowed to float silently on; accurate marks were taken, and on reaching the cliff, we pulled cautiously along its base before again taking our station far above the spot where the charming vision faded from our eyes. Every moment made me feel more and more certain of being in the exact line. Now the fly must be within five yards of the place — now within two — now within one. Can we have passed him? There is the smallest conceivable rise — a backward motion of the rod, and such a swirl! "He's got what he won't get rid of easily. That's fine! Och, but that's beautiful! Ah, master! sure there's nothing like this in ould Ireland, any way at all."

Thus spoke my faithful servant, instinctively charging his pipe, whilst a faint smile stole over his honest and sober face. Now rooting at the bottom, now rolling over the surface, again and again flying as if life depended on his speed, what a gallant fish it was! Little by little his efforts grew more laborious and less effective. Presently the broad tail which led to his destruction, scarcely possessed the power to keep that small head under water. More faintly still he fluttered from the fatal net, now it is over; nature can do no more, and like a log he is drawn slowly and steadily towards the boat; another foot and he is safe and on board. I would have walked all the way from Dublin for that one fish. "Ten pounds and a quarter! No, not quite a quarter (our clerk of weights and measures was very precise) call him ten pounds lucky. That's something like a trout." Over and over again the same course was tried, in the hope of meeting another of the same class, but in vain. At length we resigned it reluctantly, and commenced a fresh drift over the broadest part of the lake in a line with Church Island. Half way down the shore of that low rocky reef a good fish rose right ahead. Slowly the fly sailed straight towards him. "What's that?" My first thought was that Willie, who just before was sitting on the gunwale, had tumbled head-over-heels into the water. But no; there he sat, composed as ever. "He's an awful monster, master; as big as a salmon." To jerk the line out, reel sharply up, so as to ensure my companion fair play, was but the work of an instant. Had it not been for that startling plunge he might have been fast in a rock for anything I could see to the contrary. Fish have temperaments various as their captors; they are shy, bold, cowardly, volatile, sulky, or determined, and the one now under treatment combined the latter qualities in about equal proportions. For a full hour we saw nothing of him, and all this time had been drifting deeper into the rocky and shallow bay beyond the island. "Pull, pull, I'm fast! he's sat down. Oh dear, oh dear! what will I do? Pull, pull for your lives!" A few dashing strokes brought the boat over the exhausted monster; the line was free, and the battle over. There he lay on the bottom, with his great side leaning against the rock that refused him shelter. The water was barely 5 ft. deep; off went the net, on went the gaff, and then we found leisure to admire our prize. Perfect in make, exquisite in harmony of colour, in weight 13 lb. — truly he was a picture; glorious in life, beautiful in death, it may be long before his fellow is hung with such a thread. As may be imagined, all that occurred subsequently was tame. Two more, however, of 3 lb. and 5 lb. wound up the best day I ever saw with the blow line.

W Peard, *A Year of Liberty*

As showing what a first-class fisherman could do with the dry-fly in Ireland I may record that Alington told me that he had caught a hundred trout, averaging two pounds, in various rivers of the south-west in a fortnight. His best day was at Adare, where he fished for and caught nine fish, one of 3 lb. 13 oz., three of 3 lb. 10 oz., two of 2½ lb., and the rest all a little over 1½ lb., except the last, which was a 10-pound salmon caught on an alder with 3x gut.

Maurice Headlam, *Irish Reminiscences*

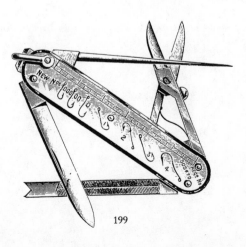

With his account of one such day let me end this chapter. It came during high water in August eight or nine years ago. Patsey (who is a painter by trade) was professionally engaged at the Grey House (of which you will read later), and on this particular morning was crossing the lake to resume his painting. Of course he had his rod along with him; when had he not? As he crossed the big shallow he saw a trout feeding. He stopped, backed to the spot he had marked, and at the very first cast hooked and killed a nice fish. By the time he had come to the house he had four trout in the boat. As he went through the stable-yard he met the master. 'Did you see any rises as you came over, Patsey?' 'I did, sir, and fine ones. Sure I killed four, they're below in the boat.' They went to see them. 'It looks like a good day; what do you think, Patsey?' 'Devil a finer, sir, have I seen these last five years; the water is an elegant colour.' They looked out over the lake. 'Never mind the painting, I'll get my rod.' They came in for lunch; duties prevented them from resuming sport for some further time, and they had to come in before dinner. But in the short time they were on the water they took between thirty and forty trout, not one of which was under one and three-quarter pounds. As it was, Patsey lamented the time wasted, and he has never ceased to regret that I had not been his companion on that great day. 'Faith, you'd ha' filled the boat — and the Master fishing with a hook broke at the barb!'

F D Barker, *An Angler's Paradise*

Sir Edward Grey, onetime British Foreign Secretary, was probably the first man to cast a dry fly on the Tipperary Suir. He thought it was wonderful fishing, although the fish were difficult. They are as difficult today.

The next reminiscence goes back to about 1880, and has to do with a river in Ireland. The first time I saw this river was late in August. There were said to be trout, and good ones, and it was believed to be possible to catch some with fly earlier in the season, when the water was in order. The river had in parts a very wide bed, which when low it did not nearly fill. The water ran in all sorts of channels between beds of bright green weeds. Here and there was a long stream with a stony bottom, free from weeds, and now and then there would be a huge pool, full of peaty-coloured water of unknown depth, in which one or two salmon lay. One could wander for miles all day about the most extraordinary variety of water. The river was full of pike, and it was said, probably with truth, that the inhabitants of the district forked trout out of the weeds in low water with various agricultural implements. But there were trout enough for dry fly fishing. Half a dozen or so might be found rising near together, and then perhaps one would have to go several hundred yards before another one was found; a little sound would be heard presently, as if a small pebble had dropped in somewhere without a splash, and heard perhaps two or three times before the rise could be seen in such a large and curious river. Then there was a difficult stalk, probably through water and weeds, with the chance of going overhead into a big hole unawares.

I was warned that at this season of the year, when the water was low, I must not expect to catch any of these fish, but I cared nothing for warnings. The trout were there, and were rising, and though I saw at once that it was a case for dry fly and for that only, I had by this time been taught to believe that any one, who could catch Winchester trout, could catch rising trout anywhere. These trout, however, at first upset my calculations. They brought me face to face with a difficulty which did not exist on the ticket water at Winchester — they were unapproachable. Never was an angler more put upon his mettle. There were trout visibly and audibly rising, which had never seen an artificial dry fly, and would probably take it at once. They were evidently also big trout. There was splendid sport to be had, and reputation and glory to be won in catching even one of them, and yet so shy were they, that I could not get my dry fly to them.

For two days they defeated me utterly. I walked and knelt and waded and laboured and perspired under an August sun without success. Some of the trout were put down by my approach, some were scared by the first waving of the rod, and some, which had been successfully stalked, turned tail and fled when the gut floated over them without even the least drag; at last, on the second evening in a fading light, I hooked a fish which went off up stream at once with a mighty rush, and came to rest somewhere out of sight at the end of a lot of line. I waded carefully up in the twilight, keeping a tight line by reeling up as I went till I was over a great bed of strong weeds. Into this one hand carefully felt its way along the casting line, and touched at last the side of a great fish. Nothing could be seen for it was getting dark, and the weeds were too thick for a landing net to be used in them. I tried with one hand to arrange a grip on the trout, and very broad and hard he felt; but at the critical moment he made the most violent commotion in the weeds and dashed off somewhere. When all was still I felt again and found in the weeds only the end of broken gut. There was nothing more to be done that evening, and I waded out and lay on the bank in the dusk. On the whole, I think that was the bitterest moment I have ever known in angling. To have come so near to success, and to have it snatched from me at the last moment, after keenness and effort had been sustained at the very highest pitch for two whole days, was more than could be borne.

But success did come afterwards, and in broad daylight; I found a place where, by wading and kneeling in the river on the shallow side, it was possible to get within reach of and *opposite* to rising trout without frightening them. Then the fly could be thrown some way above them with an underhand cast, so as not to show the rod; and being opposite and not below, I could let the fly float down a few inches on the near side of a rising trout, so that only the fly and none of the gut was seen. In this way I at last caught one or two trout, and then somehow, when the frost of failure had once broken up, it seemed more easy to succeed all over the river.

These trout were the shyest I have ever known. They were more difficult to approach and more easily scared by rod or gut than any others I ever fished for; but if the fly could be floated to a rising fish without frightening it, the fly was generally taken. On the best day that I had there I caught eleven fish. None of these weighed three pounds, but the first two were each over two pounds and three-quarters. For such shy fish really fine gut had to be used, and there were many disasters in the weeds, but also many splendid struggles fought out in pools which were far too deep for any vegetation. It was the wildest and most exciting and most fascinating dry fly fishing that I have ever had. My experience of it has only been during late August or early September, but I can imagine that in May and in June it might be the finest dry fly fishing in the United Kingdom.[1]

Sir Edward Grey, *Fly Fishing*

1. The river was the Suir, and the part of it described was at Graiguenoe, not far from Thurles. Before 1880 I do not think any one had ever fished it with a dry fly. I was never there after 1886, but I heard that the merits of the water for dry fly fishing were afterwards much appreciated by many anglers.

DANGERS AND DISASTERS

CHAPTER 8

Fishing is a dangerous sport. Water kills, but it is not the only danger. There are bulls, barbed wire, vicious dogs and midges. There are rabbitholes, hidden rocks, deep holes and other anglers. There are more obscure hazards, such as the religious obscurantism encountered by the righteous Sir Humphry Davy, or indeed the wayward hook that catches what it is not meant to catch.

Not every angler would be so sanguine as G D Luard, faced with a choice between a fish and a stick of dynamite on the Blackwater in Cork. Or indeed Maurice Headlam, waving nonchalantly from mid-river in the Tipperary Suir at a group of bloodthirsty Sinn Féiners intent on burning down the local Big House during the Troubles in the Twenties. In the days when men were men, S B Wilkinson waded torrents and refused to give in to a big salmon.

THE SABBATH DAY

Sir Humphry Davy's 'Salmonia' is the poor man's 'Compleat Angler' — dull, pretentious and wordy. Here he (almost) gets his come-uppance on a rare visit to Ireland.

Once in the north of Ireland, when a very young man, I ventured after the time of divine service to put together my rods, as I had been used to do in the Catholic districts of Ireland, and fish for sea trout in the river at Rathmelton, in pure innocence of heart, unconscious of wrong, when I found a crowd collect round me — at first I thought from mere curiosity, but I soon discovered I was mistaken; anger was their motive, and vengeance their object. A man soon came up, exceedingly drunk, and began to abuse me by various indecent terms: such as a Sabbath breaking papist, &c. It was in vain I assured him I was no papist, and no intentional Sabbath breaker; he seized my rod and carried it off with imprecations; and it was only with great difficulty, and in exciting by my eloquence the pity of some women who were present, and who thought I was an ill-used stranger, that I recovered my property.

Sir Humphry Davy, *Salmonia*

Pat did a very plucky thing on one occasion. There were several boats out, but nobody had killed a fish, although there were plenty of them in the water. We had been flogging away the greater part of the day, but the "divil a tail we saw", it was getting towards evening and the other boats were moving homewards over to Garrison. I proposed doing likewise, but Pat would not hear of it. "Wait, yer honner, till they do be all away home and the sun down behind the Dartrey hills, shure didn't I see a big fish rolling last evening when the sun was off the water, in there betune where the two rivers run in to the lough and he'll not be far away this same evening." And right Pat was; we dropped down very quietly over the spot as the last boat rounded Ross Point and nobody was witness to what happened.

I had a golden olive fly on the tail and a "Lough Gill" on the drop, and up he came directly we reached the lodge, making a tremendous ring where his tail hit the water going down. "In him" right enough, and the "Golden Olive" had done the trick; he was a sporting fish and fought hard, but his runs were getting shorter and his jumps fewer. Gradually he came nearer and nearer, the gaff was in Pat's right hand with his left hand resting on the stern of the boat, nicely balanced to deliver the stroke. Suddenly the fish made a terrific plunge right under the boat and dragged the dropper on to poor Pat's hand — the hook entered the fleshy part between the thumb and finger! It all happened like a flash. Pat never flinched. There was only one way, he seized the hook and literally tore it away from the flesh, and there seemed to be at least six inches of stretched skin before the hold gave way. It was a horrible sight and must have caused poor Pat great pain, but he did not seem to feel any; it was soon all over, another plunge and the steel went truly home and a beautiful fresh twelve pounder lay on the boards at the bottom of the boat. We felt very proud as we paddled across to Garrison. The evening was closing in rapidly, but there was still enough light to show to all the anglers collected on the bridge that we had a clean bright fish. We had to answer all sorts of questions as to where we got him, what fly, etc., all the boatmen very jealous, or "Was it on the troll I got him?" (we were not allowed to troll inside Rossinver Bay), "or maybe it was a prawn yer honner had on," etc., etc. The fish was much admired, but no one believed I got it by fair casting.

S B Wilkinson, *Reminiscences of Sport in Ireland*

G D Luard has a difficult choice to make while fishing the Cork Blackwater near Castletownroche.

To reach Reilly's you have to climb through a fence and then walk up a little over a quarter of a mile, under a picturesque farm set on a knoll and through a clump of trees awkward to negotiate with two big rods on your shoulder.

This stream, though neither long nor deep, is very pleasant to fish.

The green bank on which you stand with your left shoulder towards the river is just the right height. The stream runs fairly fast with a sort of all-over ripple, and the bottom is of gravel and round stones. A fly is best in it, and the lower you go the further out you must cast, but your fly must swing right in under your own bank. For here there are three taking spots, and a most convenient line of bushes prevents your being seen.

It is best in pretty high water, and one of my lucky spots, and if it was not so far away we should fish it more often. I once had a rather alarming experience there, which is what I really set out to describe when I began. Dick was fishing Gowra, and as the river was in good order for it, I tramped up to give Reilly's a try.

As I came out through the clump of trees and through the bramble brake on to the bank, I saw two men working in a small quarry which lies back about twenty yards from the river.

I passed the time of day with them and then began to fish. I remember I had up a small double-hooked thunder-and-lightning — I suppose the strain of subsequent anxiety impressed it on my mind.

At about the sixth cast I hooked an extremely lively fish, and at the same time one of the men shouted.

I thought for a moment it was merely his excitement at seeing a fish hooked. But he shouted again, evidently trying to attract my attention. I was annoyed, for what with the noise of the river, and my concentration on the antics of the fish, it was extremely difficult to hear. Realizing this, he strolled towards me, and what he said made me sit up.

'Listen now, Sorr,' he said. 'Tim here thinks you should know 'tis half an hour now since we put in a blasting charge and the bloody thing's hanging fire.' It was all delightfully casual. 'It might go off any time now,' he added, 'or of course it might not. There's no knowing, but I think we have it fixed.'

'Will I be all right here?' I asked with my head over my shoulder, and all the time hanging on to the fish, which had made an excursion across the river and was now trying to go down stream.

'Indeed an' you will not then,' he replied. 'The last time it threw boulders every way as big as your head; you can see some of them now on the grass beside you'; and with that they both made off into safety.

Here was a nice predicament. I could not give up the salmon. The only thing was to find what shelter I could.

Luckily the fish was pretty quiet at the moment, so I sat down on the edge of the bank and slithered into the water, which came up higher than I expected on my waders, and edged down stream, stooping as low as I could under the bank, with the knowledge that one false step would plunge me into deep water.

All the time I was playing the fish as best I could in my cramped position, and all the time half my mind was on that 'blasted' or rather unblasted quarry.

Then the fish again ran well out into the stream, and came round in a curve till he was directly below me.

That suited me in one way, as it meant that as I followed him I should gradually get more out of the direct line of fire, and nearer the protection of some big trees and bushes which grew thickly on the bank.

He was now in a sort of backwater, but still dropping down stream. If once he got into the strong current near the sheltering trees he would go right away from me and it was too deep to follow. I therefore held him hard, and still stooping low hurried down with the current, reeling myself up to him as it were as I went. The last bit I almost ran, if it could be called running in such deep water.

By holding my rod bent nearly double over my shoulder I was now just within reach. My long gaff was ready in my hand. Putting on all the strain I could, I held him stationary for a moment, and pulled it home, just as the strong water was beginning to lift my feet.

Somehow I struggled to the bank; somehow through brambles, thorns, and bushes I heaved myself, my rod and the fish out, and with it still on the gaff fairly ran through the trees until I felt safe.

The explosion did not take place till ten o'clock that night. But 'sure there was no knowing'.

G D Luard, *Fishing Fortunes and Misfortunes*

Maurice Headlam finds himself in a tricky situation in mid-stream on the Suir.

Though Clarke's Water had, nearly all of it, those low banks which are so pleasant for dry-fly fishing, there was a deep high-banked stretch below where the local anglers extracted enormous trout with the natural mayfly dapped — often, I understood, cross-lining. At the top of this stretch there ran in a tributary, the Clodiagh, on which "Arny" FitzHerbert (who had made the record bag of wood-pigeons, at Lord de Vesci's at Abbeyleix where his father was agent) had once caught, in mayfly time, eight three-pounders in one day.

At my last visit to Graiguenoe in 1921, after I had officially left Ireland, I determined to try this lower water if the mayfly was well up. The country was in a very disturbed state. I travelled to Thurles with Sir Charles Barrington who lived near Limerick, and we talked fishing. Afterwards I heard that, when he reached home, he found that his daughter had been murdered by Sinn Féiners on her way to a tennis party.

When I arrived at Graiguenoe I was told that bullets had been passing over the house all day: the Sinn Féiners were attacking the police barracks on the hill behind the house. I thought that the river would be the safest place, so at once put on my waders, in order to be below the line of fire. I had always fished alone, but several anglers had been kidnapped by Sinn Féiners and this time I took with me a small boy to carry my bag: I thought that, if the same thing happened to me, there would be someone who would be able to convey news of the incident. When we got to the lower river there was little or no fly, and no rise, either in the main river, or the Clodiagh. But I met a party of men with brand-new bandoliers and rifles though little other attempt at uniform. I was crossing the river at the time, with the small boy on my back, and shouted a greeting, thinking they were the "Black and Tans" about whom certain circles in London were getting up an agitation. They answered civilly enough and walked on. When I got back to Graiguenoe I was told that they were not Black and Tans but the Sinn Féin patrol come down from the mountains, and that I was lucky not to have been shot or taken prisoner.

I never saw Graiguenoe again, for it was burned down shortly afterwards, happily when the Clarkes were away.

Maurice Headlam, *Irish Reminiscences*

High in the upland of Iar Connaught lies a small lake which communicates with the main river by a bog stream often less than a foot wide and half buried under coarse grass. White trout find their way up this runnel and into the lake which is mostly unfishable because of a growth of rushes spearing up from the bottom, sometimes dense, sometimes sparse, but always sufficiently close together to prevent any working of a fly. At one spot however a canal of open water, about 12 yards wide, stretches out from the shore and then turns sharply to the left. In shape this clear area is that of an inverted capital L the long arm being about 35 yards and the short arm about 15. At the shore end a big granite boulder, about six feet high but climbable, provides a casting platform. Usually a white trout or two could be picked up here, mostly herling not exceeding a pound in weight. But this fish was no herling. It took some ten yards from shore and without a second's delay shot off for the far end of the canal. A biggish white trout is away the moment he is hooked and the first twenty yards of his dash is just one electric streak. My fish made straight for the rushes that rose like a wall at the far end of the open water canal. If he reached them he was safe. If I tried to stop him too brusquely there was the probability of a break. Very gentle checking slowed him perceptibly but he showed no sign of stopping. When he was two yards from the rushes I took a chance and clamped my finger on the reel plate. Only two yards to go! He fought relentlessly to gain his asylum while I held on not giving an inch. It must have been two minutes or more before the strain suddenly relaxed and I was able to recover a few yards of line. But now he was off up the shorter left arm of the open water putting a long stretch of rush studded water between us. Owing to the height of the boulder on which I was standing it was possible to keep line and cast above the rushes which were not very tall, but there seemed no way by which to bring him back into the main canal. I examined the area of rushes.

Yes, there was one place where they grew more sparsely. A tired fish might, with luck, be skull-hauled head above water through the obstacles and back into the long arm, but the problem was how to keep him in open water till he was sufficiently exhausted to make the experiment worth trying. If he chose to run towards me and into the near rushes he would be free in a few seconds. Luck was with me for, by keeping a steady strain I ensured that he would pull against the strain and towards the further fringes of the rushes. A series of short spurts varied by jumps further wearied him. Now he was opposite the sparse area of rushes and the attempt must be made. The first stage was to get his head above water which meant lowering my rod top as much as possible without fouling the line and then raising it to its full extension with my hand high above my head. Good, he was showing on the surface. Now it was a question of stripping in the line so rapidly that he became bewildered and for the moment ceased resistance, all the while steering him away from the denser growth. More than once the dropper touched projecting spikes but did not take hold and now, at last, he was in the main arm and completely under control. I could see him clearly, a fresh run fish of between three and four pounds. At the base of my boulder crouched the ghillie, a young man of 18 already an expert boatman and trained to net a fish by keeping the net well sunk in the water till the fish was drawn over it. I glanced down. There was the net a foot below the surface. In came the fish unresisting in a steady glide till at the last moment he saw me, checked and made to turn back. It was too much for my ghillie who took a step into the water and scooped wildly. The fish balanced on the edge of the net half in and half out, fell back catching the dropper in the rushes, and was gone.

The lesson is to net your fish yourself and this normally I would have done, but for the difficulty of climbing down from the six foot high boulder with a fish at the end of the line. The second lesson is never, never, allow your ghillie to scoop at a fish. Some boatmen are expert at landing a fish in this way but it is always more risky than allowing the angler to draw the fish well over the net and then raise it steadily.

T H Kingsmill Moore, *A Man May Fish*

S B Wilkinson in the thick of things on the River Erne in Fermanagh.

It was one day on the river, good for nothing except butterflies or bathing, not a breath of air, and everything looked like copper, the river reflecting this tint looked more like red oil than water as it passed from pool to pool; my ghillie, Terry O'Ge, agreed with me that it was useless to attempt fishing. I had been some time sitting up on the shaded bank at Moss Row smoking and dreaming and thinking of the fine clean fish that Dr. Peard describes as having killed on this throw in his *Year of Liberty.* I was asleep when my ghillie took up the rod and went down the few feet to the water.

"What in the world are you going to do, Terry?"

"Well, yer honour, sorra a fish you'll ever get wid yer fly on dry land."

"True for you, Terry. You fish and I will eat my sandwiches."

There was something about the fly that Terry did not like, and he sat down to choose another. By the time he had pleased himself I had finished and was thinking of something to wash down the sandwiches and cake when up came the head waterkeeper. We commenced to chat. Terry had waded out and was fishing very carefully, the fly falling on the oily surface as lightly as a feather, about ten feet below where we were fishing. Suddenly I noticed a displacement of the water, not broken, nor a sign of a rise, but an almost imperceptible bulging of the water. I shouted to Terry that he had *moved* a fish, and the waterkeeper agreed. Terry had seen nothing; he was too near the water's level, so we shouted to him to draw in his line by hand. He now began to fish the throw again, letting out a little by degrees; now the last yard had gone out and the fly was at the same spot where we thought the fish had moved. Up went Terry's rod, and he was into our friend. He had taken the fly deep in the water so we could not form even an idea as to size. It's a horrible bit of wading, big blocks of rock and deep holes. I would not go down until I had finished my pipe. Terry was roaring for help, still I did not go till at last his cries became so piteous that the waterkeeper said he would go out of his mind if I did not take the rod. I took in as much as I could of my waders with the belt round my waist in case of a dip, and went down into the water with the gaff. I took the rod from Terry, giving the gaff to him in exchange. The fish felt light to me, and Terry when asked agreed that it was not very large. I proceeded to lead the fish up to the limestone flag, and I had then to get over a low wall. For over a hundred yards he had been perfectly quiet, leading along without the slightest objection.

"Keep down a bit, Terry, and I will try and swing him into you."

The words were hardly out of my mouth when this supposed small one of little account had turned round and the pace that we had to keep at, first on the flag, after that through the bad part, I never remember anything faster. We had no means of telling the pace, but it was very considerably faster than I had ever to follow a fish before. I looked for a pause at the lodge where he was hooked, but no, on he went, and I was very nearly out of line. If I could only make the little grassy bank at the end of the wood I would be all right. Alas, here it was that Terry let me down badly. I had tripped several times, but had been steadied by him; but now, not only did he fail to hold me up, but fell on the top of me! I kept the point of my rod pointing upwards, and made desperate efforts to get up, using — well, we will call it language — at Terry, he calling on every Saint in the calendar, the water pouring down my neck and into my waders. I made one last heave and flung Terry off me, and a still further effort and I had reached the grassy bank. Terry was only a second or two behind; we soon had all the bagging line reeled up and found our fish gone over to the south bank and rather higher up than we were, about eighty yards away. It was a big job he had given us; we could not get right across, so had to keep bullying him and not give him time to lie down; we kept moving him by slow degrees and took advantage of any spot that we could wade. I had very nearly had enough to it and would willingly have been rid of the brute: it must have been over two hours the fight had lasted. He was still fighting well, but I noticed his runs were not made with such vigour, and yet I thought it hopeless that we should ever be able to get him over to us; then by some lucky manoeuvre he had crossed into a stream that brought him to our side again! Now there was hope. I had him nearer, and presently under the point of my rod and never let him get very far away again. The end was getting nearer; he had already been on his side; Terry was down below watching for his chance; nearer, no not quite; he had floundered out again, evidently not liking the look of Terry; again he turned on his side, and I was able to give Terry another chance and he took it well, walking out of the water with the fish on the gaff and with a tight hold of his tail to stop his wriggling; a crack on his snout ended a terrific fight. He was a red fish in good condition with a big crummogue already indenting his upper jaw. Weight: twenty-three pounds. An excellent kipper. We produced the flask and each had a good three fingers, and deserved them. Tell that to the prohibitionists! The waterkeeper said when it was all over that it was as good as going to prayers to listen to Terry calling on the Saints. All the same, we might very easily have been drowned in that horrible bit of wading.

S B Wilkinson, *Reminiscences of Sport in Ireland*

ENVOI

WHAT KILLS FISH?

Irish angling waters face a dismaying future viewed from a dismal present. Despite all the earnest endeavour, the goodwill and the exercise of reason and commonsense, the quality of our game angling waters goes down and down. Our great western lakes are under threat from the spread of roach; our seatrout fisheries are in diseased disarray; our rivers, lakes and ponds are increasingly polluted, over-fished and poorly-managed.

What kills fish — and this extract soberly outlines just that — also kills fishing. It is a sombre note on which to end what, to me, has been a happy book to compile.

Fish kills resulting from pollution may be caused by suffocation, toxic substances in the water, mechanical injury or a combination of these and other factors, including natural ones. When suffocation occurs it is due to oxygen depletion caused by the decomposition of organic substances discharged in wastes. Most common among such wastes are improperly treated sewage, animal slurry, cannery and milk processing wastes.

Sometimes fish are killed by mechanical injury. In many cases the injuries are obvious, especially when the fish have passed through turbines or pumps. Underwater explosions may produce fatal internal injuries, but extensive kills occur only when fish are concentrated in the immediate area of the detonation.

The presence of materials toxic to fish is usually the cause of the most spectacular and serious kills. Certain chemicals used by industry are very toxic. Metals such as copper, zinc and chrome are lethal even at low concentrations and when they occur with cyanide from metal plating or metal finishing industries, serious fish kills can result. Many chemical processes produce wastes which are very acid or very alkaline. While these may kill fish, they may also greatly increase the toxicity of substances which would otherwise be harmless.

Normally, when waste is discharged continuously into a stream, it flows downstream with the current, becoming less concentrated as the processes of dilution and natural purification reduce its strength. When waste discharge is intermittent, a block of the polluting material may move downstream as an entity and, when strong enough, kill for a considerable distance. Occasionally liquid waste in road-transport containers may be accidentally or purposely dumped into rivers.

Aside from industrial pollution, the inadvertent or thoughtless disposal of pesticides in watercourses is a potential source of fish mortality. The rinsing of agricultural spray equipment, careless pumping of stream water into spray tanks and dumping unused portions of pesticide into a stream may have serious consequences.

Often fish will move to escape pollution, either swimming ahead of it or dodging into tributary streams where they remain until the unfavourable conditions have passed. There are, however, substances such as phenol which fish do not recognize as dangerous and do not avoid. Moreover, a few substances such as chlorine which are directly harmful attract fish so that they swim towards an increasing concentration and their ultimate destruction.

Institute of Industrial Research and Standards: *Guide to the Investigation of Fish Kills*